ABHYV I JAHAN

Love, Profit aur Dhokha

On managing, growing, and transforming your small business

Contents

II Grow

III   Transform

Tu Kaun

Who I am

I am a lot like you. And a bit like *that* person you know. Seriously, this is not an attempt to be relatable (although I've read that it helps sell more books).

I'm the person who gets a gym membership under the delusion that the act of becoming a member will rid me of my inherent laziness and lack of willpower. I stop working out after a week, reinstall Swiggy and Zomato, eat till I can start feeling guilty, and then curse the apps for being so addictive. I'm the person working in a domain far from my field of study, hoping to draw connections between real life and academic studies to justify the amount of time and money spent on my education. I'm the one who started running a business because I felt entrepreneurship was my calling and realized too late how bloody difficult it is. Sound familiar?

I'm 29 years old. That's a little older than when you realize that your seeming uniqueness was a delusion and you're just as boring as everybody else. It hurts to realize how commonplace I really am. I'm also at the age when I'm too old to be called a prodigy and too young to be called an expert. I am always second-guessing myself, sharing suggestions under the guise that it came from someone else, and silently celebrating when the suggestion proves helpful. I'm pitiful!

I have come to realize, however, that I have certain personality deficiencies that have helped me as an entrepreneur.

- I am too stubborn and shameless to stop trying.
- I can't overcome the feeling of being a failure, to the extent that it fuels my stubbornness.
- I am willing to pay the price the above attitude demands.

The price? I'll let Charles Bukowski answer:

> "If you're going to try, go all the way. Otherwise, don't even start.
>
> This could mean losing girlfriends, wives, relatives and maybe even your mind. It could mean not eating for three or four days. It could mean freezing on a park bench. It could mean jail. It could mean derision. It could mean mockery—isolation.
>
> Isolation is the gift. All the others are a test of your endurance, of how much you really want to do it. And, you'll do it, despite rejection and the worst odds. And it will be better than anything else you can imagine. If you're going to try, go all the way.
>
> There is no other feeling like that. You will be alone with the gods, and the nights will flame with fire. You will ride life straight to perfect laughter. It's the only good fight there is."

I realized the above when entrepreneurship happened to me. In late 2017, my parents invested in a manufacturing company.

They invested the majority of their savings from working for over 30 years. They got into a commercial understanding with the owners of the company to become silent partners. In a few months, it became clear that the original directors were driving the company into the ground through mismanagement and malpractices. In an attempt to secure my family's interests, I took over as the CEO of the company in early 2018.

This company, basically, was the worst kind of startup. Only two years old, it didn't have much in terms of internal systems and processes, market reputation, or business model. On top of that, it had huge debt, was making heavy losses every month, and customers had started leaving. For the first six months, I was a startled duck trying to deal with issues I hadn't thought of ever thinking about.

Over two years, though, the company became profitable, survived an economic crisis while our competitors shut shop, created a firm position as one of the top 3 manufacturers of our product segment in the country, is applying for 3 patents, and is in talks with foreign manufacturers for a first-of-its-kind JV in India. I was able to turn around the small business.

There are many definitions of small businesses. I like the one below:

> *A business is small if it continues to face life-threatening issues, with every passing day it demands more and more of your time, the problems keep multiplying, and there seems to be no end.*

No matter how much revenue you make. You could be a startup making a lakh per year or an established player with a revenue of many crores per year. If the above applies to your business, for the purpose of this book, it's a small business.

About a year and a half into running the business, we seemed to have reached an inflection point. Issues seemed more and more manageable, it demanded less time from me with each passing day, the problems seemed to be going away, and we could see an end to this stage and a beginning to the next. We started not being a small business.

It was completely unexpected. From the company demanding 16 hours a day (I used to live at the factory), every day, to 4 hours a day of my time two years later; I couldn't believe it when it happened. And I didn't know *how*. I know I had dreamt about such a time. So, I started reviewing my steps, trying to figure out what worked.

Why I wrote this book

Because I am selfish, narcissistic and egomaniacal. In my defence, any author who says differently is lying. Or any entrepreneur, for that matter.

But I wish I didn't *have* to feel like a failure as many times as I did. I wish there were fewer occasions, when I *had* to keep digging deeper, through the night, to find enough stubbornness to get to work the next day. I wish I didn't *have* to feel ashamed by my mistakes as much as I did.

Running a business is tough enough by itself. There were problems specific to the business I was running. Those were problems only I could find solutions to. But I wish someone had told me what I've learnt about common problems that almost all small businesses face. Problems to which solutions exist but not enough people talk about them. No one worth listening to, anyway (there comes the narcissism). People who know these answers keep them hidden away, using it as a competitive advantage.

I started writing this book as a personal journal of things I'd learned that worked out, hoping to use it as a competitive advantage too. In the process of writing this, though, I found that most of my learnings came from people who were willing to share them. Not very promptly, for sure. But they did share. In an attempt to feel less selfish, I decided to share too.

So, this book. It's a series of rants and sob stories. Mixed with insights and learnings. With a dash of hope that reading this will help reduce the number of times you feel too ashamed about a dumb mistake or too hurt to go to sleep or too much like a failure.

Kaiko

Why you should buy this book

If the title and cover page didn't get you, and you're too heartless to relate to the tear-jerker that is *Tu Kaun*; you fall under one of three categories.

1. You're standing at a bookstore, trying to impress someone by pretending to read this. They *know* you haven't read a book since you left school. The only way to convince them otherwise is to buy the book. That shows commitment to reading. Can't be faked.

2. You're at a friend's place, hoping to be more than friends with them or someone else. So, you picked up the book in an attempt to seem thoughtful. Well, you *know* you need a common topic to discuss with this person. It's the only good excuse to call them. And don't think of borrowing the book. That's pathetic. Order it on Amazon, read a few chapters, and tell them how the book (which you obviously associate with that person) has changed your life.

3. If you're still not convinced, you're actually not my target

audience. Doesn't that make you feel left out? Buy the book! I am an entrepreneur with a fledgling business. I could really use the money. Think of it as a donation! Right, that's as low as I can go. Buy it, don't buy it, I don't care.

Shukriya

I have no one to thank for the writing of this book. I did it all by myself. A few people gave good feedback but, come on, I could have figured those out by myself. So, Shruti and Karishma, thanks for nothing. I love you guys.

I have a lot of people to thank, though, for continuing to stand by (read: tolerate) me as I zigzag my way through work and life:

- Ashna, my sister, for being my emotional backbone. I love you ten thousand.
- My parents for their mentorship and irrational belief in me.
- My team, who put their trust in a guy who was visibly out of his depth.
- A special mention for Aman, Sudeep, Alok, Rajnish, Arshad Sir, Santosh, Sanjeet, Mishra ji, Vijay, and Apurva from my team, who continue to tolerate a guy who puts them on a wild goose chase with a new idea every week. Luckily, a few of those worked out. Most of what I have learned, I learned through them.
- Pardesi *kaka* and Buddhu *kaka* for keeping me fed through times when eating seemed like an unwelcome distraction. And continuing to do so when overeating took over.
- Harshit and Manish for being there even when they didn't understand.
- Prof. Anil Gupta of IIM Ahmedabad for sharing the follow-

ing lines with me. They got me through some desperately hard and lonely nights.

"Safeena nazar-e-toofan hua
   Thak gaye baazu
   Chala jata hoon
   Mauz-e-havadis ko kinara samajh kar."

"My boat has met a storm
   My arms are exhausted
   But I keep moving on
   Believing that the next wave of destruction is actually
the shore."

I

Manage

1

Data kitthe

On measuring important parameters for your business

"You can't improve what you don't measure"

The above is a paraphrasing of Peter Drucker's original quote, "If you can't measure it, you can't improve it." Since I am yet to come across an aspect that *can't* be measured, I find the paraphrased version more useful.

As with most small businesses, the company I took over suffered from dearth of data. No one knew exactly how much money was spent every month, whether the company was profitable, how much raw material was used for producing 1 ton of finished product, how much waste was generated. The list goes on. The answers to these questions varied depending on whom I spoke with. And answers could be very colourful.

I once asked my production supervisor how much slag was produced when melting steel scrap (to figure out what is called the *burning loss*). The conversation went as follows:

> *Supervisor:* Sir, depend karta hai. (Sir, it depends.)
> *Me:* Kispe? (On what?)
> *Supervisor:* Aap pe. (On you.)
> *Me:* Matlab? (What do you mean?)
> *Supervisor:* Aap kaisa maal mangvate hain galaane ke liye us hisaab se burning loss hoga. Heavy maal me kam hoga, light me zaada, teena me sabse zaada. (Depending on the kind of raw material you get, the burning loss could be low or high. If it's heavy material, burning loss will be low; if it's light material, burning loss will be high.)
> *Me:* Light me kitna hoga? (How much is the burning loss in light material?)
> *Supervisor:* Sir, depend karta hai. (Sir, it depends.)
> *Me:* Kispe? (On what?)
> *Supervisor:* Maal dene waale pe. (On the supplier.)
> *Me:* Matlab? (What do you mean?)
> *Supervisor:* Scrap wala agar acha light maal dega toh kam hoga, maal me agar mitti ya dust hoga toh zaada burning loss hoga. (If the supplier gets good quality light material, burning loss will be low. If it has dust and other impurities, burning loss will be high.)
> *Me:* Mitti wale maal me kitna hoga? (How much is it for light material with impurities?)
> *Supervisor:* Sir, depend karta hai. (Sir, it depends.)

That recursive loop broke only when my headache got unbearable. In a quiet moment, though, I realised that without answering my question, he had given me insights into everything that needed to be measured in the process of scrap procurement and melting. Similar incidents happened in almost all functions of the factory and I got a rich set of parameters that needed to be measured. I had won, or so I thought.

I quickly found out that knowing what to measure is the easy part, measuring is tough. Let me clarify further, *getting people to measure is tough*. Getting people to measure regularly is even tougher. The headache started to come back.

With automation in industries, most of the data collection and processing has been sorted out. But not for small businesses. *Smart Factory* solutions are expensive and majorly cater to greenfield (new) projects. Solutions for existing factories are few and almost none for small manufacturing units.

I wish I had a simple solution to this problem. The only one that worked was dogged persistence. It became my daily routine to ask for reports on production, maintenance, sales, dispatch, and other aspects; then I would sit down with each team to review the information asking the relevant people for justifications when there was a red flag. We would then take corrective actions. Over time, this process got instilled such that reports started being generated without being asked for. That was a big achievement until I hit another roadblock- false data.

False data is an interesting monster. It looks so ordinary, so average, so unassuming. In fact, that is its biggest strength.

Someone somewhere didn't do their job right. No bother. They have reports of the last 30 days. The lazy ones would put in the number from the previous day. The smart ones would calculate an average of values of the past many days and change numbers slightly. I was at wit's end but this, luckily, has a less tedious solution. That is when I figured out there was a corollary to Drucker' quote:

> *You can't trust what you don't measure by more than one way*

Let me give you an example. Our production contractor earns money by how much scrap has been melted over the month. We have a 3-ton furnace, which means that every cycle of melting should melt a little over 3 tons of scrap (accounting for burning losses). At the end of the month, he creates an invoice based on the total number of melting cycles. The problem was that we didn't know how much scrap was actually being melted in the furnace. Those with experience of working in a steel plant will confirm that weighing steel scrap during production is unfeasible. This would give me nightmares because if the contractor decided to melt less scrap per cycle (to save on his cost of labour), it would mean higher costs for lower production.

To solve this, we started calculating total melting production through various methods, besides the total number of melting cycles per month:

1. Scrap purchase quantity and inventory: The difference between opening and closing stock would be equal to total scrap melted.

2. Quantity of additives used and final chemistry: Melting scrap to produce steel requires specific quantities of certain additives to be added to achieve the chemistry of the steel produced. The two data points can be used to calculate the total quantity of steel produced and, thereby, the quantity of scrap melted.

3. Electricity consumed: This was slightly more tricky as there is no clear mathematical formula. So, I put a couple of my trusted guys near the furnace to ensure that a full load was being melted and note down the corresponding units of electricity consumed. Over a few weeks, we had generated enough data to know how much electricity would be consumed per melting cycle. The number of units consumed can then be used to back-calculate how much scrap would have been melted. Lesser scrap being melted would show as lower number of units consumed.

Doing this not only helped us make sure that the correct amount of payment was made to the contractor but also highlighted red flags on a cycle-to-cycle basis. We've used the same principle of multimethod validation (sounds so fancy!) for accounting, unit economics, quality assurance, maintenance, and other aspects. And the headaches have reduced.

2

Aamdani athanni, kharcha rupaiya

On financial management and unit economics

There's quite a lot of debate about *whether* startups should focus on unit economics and profitability. If you live under a rock or have the good sense to not follow that debate, below are a few of your favourite startups and the losses they made in 2019 (from various sources found through a simple Google search).

- Uber- $8.5 bn
- Ola Cabs- Rs. 2593 Crore
- Oyo- Rs. 2834 Crore
- AirBnB- $335 mn
- Flipkart- Rs. 3836.8 Crore

I don't know enough about their business strategy to comment on whether this is a good sign or not. It also helps to not be an investor. I can say confidently, though, that the large majority of small businesses cannot afford such a business strategy. They'd jump ship.

Small business owners range from owning a *paan* shop to a small factory. They have low access to capital and credit. A red mark, however small, on their balance sheet further reduces their credit worthiness. So, banks will not support them when they most need it. This creates a downward spiral that ends in a common story beginning with, "My father *had* a business.." The story goes on with tales of how things seemed great in the beginning and then debt kept piling up, and finally the family lost most of its wealth paying off the debt.

You would think that because loss can be greatly damaging for the whole family and cause generations to suffer its impact, small business owners would be more cautious and knowledge-able about handling money. They aren't. Fallacies that apply to 'innovative' entrepreneurs, also apply to small business owners.

1. *If I build it, they will come*- Quite common with startups who believe that if they build a product good enough, people will buy it. Small business owners' version of this fallacy is that if they own a business, customers will line up, and income will shoot up. With little knowledge of business models, financial planning, marketing strategy, etc, they are most gullible to the *survivorship bias*. The key difference being that 'tech entrepreneurs' try to maximise differentiation. *A food delivery app worked out great for that company. How about I made an app for delivering every item shops can offer? And made sure it was hyperlocal? And you get free soap with every order of candy!*

With most other entrepreneurs, the motivation is to maximize similarity. They see a local success story and want to follow every step exactly. It's no surprise, then, that entire markets are filled with non differentiable shops selling pretty much the same stuff. E.g. An entire area dedicated to selling sarees and 200 shops to meet the same need or cigarette and *paan* shops lined up one after the other right outside a mall.

2. *Put in more money-* The quintessential *sunk costs fallacy* that makes people believe that pumping more capital into the business will solve all inherent issues. This makes business people increasingly more debt-ridden. When the bank stops supporting them, they raise funds from unsecured creditors, who charge insane interest rates and are often of dubious character. When finally the ship sinks, the effects are disastrous because the entrepreneur, in most cases, exhausts their personal and family income to help the business survive.

Both of the above applied to varying degrees when my family decided to invest in this business. And we faced the brunt for it.

I observed an interesting phenomenon, though. You know this. The failure rate of businesses run by the *bania* community are much lower than average. I had been brought up with an image of *banias* as heartless profit mongers. Well, now I was one of them. Without the requisite skills. Lack of financial literacy and discipline among entrepreneurs is neither new nor undocumented. I was financially illiterate and undisciplined.

Nothing preceding the moment I took charge of the factory had prepared me to manage the economics of running a company.

Almost everything I've learned about unit economics and financial management came from spending time with Gujarati and Marwari uncles, I like to call the *B Gang*. When I first moved to the rural town where the factory is based, I was introduced to a few seasoned businessmen in the area. This was great for my learning, not so much for my liver. The only way to spend time with them and get unreserved advice was to join their twice-weekly, heavy drinking sessions. I did that for almost 3 months, before moving to a fortnightly then monthly schedule, and finally bowing out with respect.

Following were the main lessons:

1. *Kitto aayo, kitto gayo*: For the first three months of running the factory, I actually didn't know and, idiotically, didn't care whether we were making a profit or loss and how much. When other problems started getting resolved and the bank balance started dwindling (happens very quickly in a factory), I was hit with the realization of what I didn't know.

   I started reading about how financial accounting is done. I pored over online resources and books but just couldn't figure out how to start. I would read, feel dyslexic, bang my head on the desk, get a coffee, smoke, repeat. When I brought this up at the B Gang 'meeting', they looked at me like I was a homeless puppy, desperately in need of a blanket and a smack for being so stupid.

One of them turned to me and said, "*Beta, ye chittha leyo. Aur likho– kitto aayo, kitto gayo (Son, take this piece of paper and write, how much came in and how much went out).*" And that was it. The start of our financial accounting was on pieces of paper. Once we started doing that and got the hang of it, we used Excel and came up with our own ways of structuring the data to make more sense to us. Eventually, we started using an online accounting software and creating MIS reports.

2. *Hisaab ka pakka*: This one actually came from my parents. Every expense and every payment to be recovered, however small, must be accounted for. It's easy to not account for coffee and snacks or the Rs. 10,000 still remaining with a customer who paid the remaining Rs. 10 lakh. But it's a slippery path. These expenses tend to creep up on you and bite you when you're most vulnerable.

What the B Gang taught me were discipline and *takada* (the art of repeatedly asking for payment). I discuss *takada* in *Takada With A Twist.* I would frequently hear one person come in late to the 'meeting' saying, "*Hisaab me der ho gyo (Got stuck with accounting).*" And everyone else would look at him approvingly. At the end of the day, each member of the B Gang would spend time, as long as it took, to match accounts. It's not uncommon to hear someone say, about people like those in the B Gang, "*Vo hisaab ka bada pakka hai (He is very good with money).*"

3. *Galle me kitna hai*: A lot of small business owners sell their

products in cash. A common phrase they use is, *"Galle me kitna hai (How much is in the drawer)?"* The B Gang checks their *galla* multiple times a day. Sometimes, they'd call a relative during the 'meeting' to recheck. This is an important principle in business- always know how much cash you have; in the drawer, under your mattress or the company bank account. Knowing the company bank balance at all times allows me to plan in advance for future expenses and ensure that I receive my payments in time to maintain the requisite balance.

4. *Nakad abhi, udhar nahi*: Credit cycles are a terror for SMEs and the policy of a 'cash discount' is common. What the B Gang knows clearly is that a rupee in hand is worth one and a half in the customer's hand. This policy applies to B2B products that usually sell on credit. If my customer pays me today, I can use that money to make more material and supply to more customers. If they pay me after a certain duration, my working capital gets reduced and I bear the interest on the money.

This usually becomes a conundrum because customers buying on credit generally pay a higher amount for it. The extra margin seems too lucrative to let go. And sometimes, you shouldn't. In most cases though, that money can be used multiple times to sell to other customers providing a lower margin but instant payment. Your margin multiplies with the number of times you use the same amount to produce and sell. This is called working capital rotation.

E.g. A customer agrees to pay you Rs. 100 for a product

but will pay in 3 months, while another customer will pay you only Rs. 50 but instantly. Now, assume that it costs you Rs. 40 to make the product. In the first case, the profit margin is Rs. 60 versus only Rs. 10 in the second case. The decision seems like a no-brainer. However, selling to the first customer means that Rs. 40 is out of your bank account and can no longer be used for paying salaries, electricity bills, or buying more raw material. However, **if** your sales cycle allows you to sell a product every ten days, selling to the second customer and using the money to sell to more like them, will allow you to generate a profit of Rs. 90 in the same 3 months.

It also allows money to stay in the bank longer so that expenses can be met in time. The second option has started looking good, right? It's not uncommon to hear about 'profitable' companies that ran out of cash. Profit is a concept only validated by cash. Cash is king and the *B Gang* has used this principle to create sustainable growth for decades.

5. *Jeb daliddar dil hai samundar*: This one comes easily after the above. The sooner you get payments the better. The later you make payments the better, unless you pay a penalty for late payments. I was once sitting with one of the B Gang members in his office when one of his suppliers came in to ask for payment. He was seated, given *chai* and snacks, asked about his family and pretty much everything under the sun, then given a cheque for half the amount with regret, "*Abhi itna hi hai (We only have this much right now).*" I knew the B Gang well enough to know they were

wildly cash rich. But holding on to money for as long as possible just makes good business sense.

Now that you know what the *B Gang* does well, let me tell you what they're not so good at- financial projections. And I don't mean the crazy stuff that pops up when you do a Google search or the 1000-rows long excel sheet your CA showed you. I mean planning in such a way that allows you to make financially intelligent decisions for your business.

Everything I know about this comes from the book, *Romancing The Balance Sheet* by Anil Lamba. He rightly says, "..there is no such thing as a non-Finance person. It's a misconception that Finance Management happens in the Finance department." Don't go by the title. It's not a textbook on understanding the nitty-gritty of a balance sheet, although he does cover significant aspects of that too. The book, for me as a person running a small business, provided simple ways to think about finance, simple calculations that helped me predict (with data) and plan (with quite some accuracy) how much money we would make or lose in different situations. It helped me come up with possible solutions to such scenarios and be better prepared when they presented themselves.

Buy the book. The RoI is off the chart and the *leverage effect* is exponential. Don't know what I am talking about? Buy the book!

I'll say this though:

All lives end. All hearts are broken. And all plans fail.

So don't get too attached to your plans and projections. The only good plan is to have lots of plans. Try to simulate as many scenarios as possible and come up with potential solutions to each. In late 2018, we were doing really well. The company just had its first profitable month since I took over, achieved record sales, and we had plans to increase sales by another 20% in the coming 3 months. In early 2019, the automotive industry (our primary customer) started declining. Soon after, it went into free fall. Everything we had planned for went down the drain.

What helped us is discussed in *Ek Chutki Innovation Ki Keemat*. But that was a hard lesson. Murphy's Law states that if something can go wrong, it will. With planning,

> *Something you planned for **might** go wrong. Something you didn't plan for **will** go wrong.*

3

Takada With A Twist

On the art of asking for money

The *B Gang*, as already mentioned, is very particular about not selling on credit. In fact, small business owners, selling B2C, are so particular about this that they have very interesting quotes outside their shops:

> "Rahul Gandhi ke pradhaan mantri banne tak udhaar bandh hai (No credit until Rahul Gandhi becomes the Prime Minister)"

> "Udhaar bas 80-90 saal ke logon ko milega, wo bhi unke maata pita se pooch ke (Credit will be given only to 80-90 year olds, and only after speaking to their parents)"

What small business owners know is that selling products on

credit invariably leads to *takada*. *Takada* is the "art of asking for money". This art is never devoid of friction. Everytime you call for money, you create more friction. No one likes to be called for payment reminders, especially those who have no intention of paying anytime soon.

To deal with this issue, which is inevitable in B2B businesses, the *B Gang* follows some rules:

1. *Just do it*: *Takada* is more uncomfortable for the person asking for money than the one who owes it. With every extra call, your ego takes a bigger hit. Also, you run the risk of antagonising the customer who then starts ignoring you completely. In such situations, it is common for business owners to think of the right time to call, the right frequency, the tone, and a multitude of other things.

   The *B Gang* instead just does it. They don't wait for anything to be *right*, they just call. Next, they will send someone to the customer's office with the sole instruction of sitting there until the payment is made. Sometimes, consecutively for days. Next, they will visit the customer themselves and sit with the highest authority they have access to. They keep at it until the payment is released. It's pure persistence.

2. *Kaise hoga*: When you read this, imagine it being said in a voice that's a cross between Om Puri's deep baritone and the helpless cries of a kitten. *Kaiissseee hogaaa?* This question represents pure discontentment, unaffected by the outcome of *takada*. The customer decides to pay in

a month? Not good enough. It'll take a week? Could have been sooner. Will be done tomorrow? Arrrgh. The customer is clearing dues today and paying an advance for the next two orders? *Kaiisseeee hogggaaa!*

The aim is to make the customer feel terrible about not having signed off all their property in your name in lieu of may be buying some material from you in the future. This is a strategy of creating psychological associations. Everytime the customer thinks of not paying you yet, they should be reminded of how terrible it felt last time. And the time before that.

3. *Mithai mangvaye hain*: The *B Gang* is adept at invoking the principle of reciprocity. At different times, as frequently as possible, they will send gifts to their customers. These gifts are rarely high in value but have great significance emotionally. They will call their customer to share that they recently visited a very famous *mandir* too far for any sane person to go, did a long *puja*, and are sending *prasad* from the *puja*.

Soon after, sometimes before, the *prasad* reaches the customer, the *B Gang* receives notification of payment being made. Every time a gift is sent, it is either connected to family or God and is always bound by the perception of how hard it was to get the gift (long distance, arduous journey, long duration, you get the point). More often than not, the gifts are procured without the *B Gang* having left their office. If they are from somewhere else, crucial details about how it was a greatly enjoyable holiday for the

B Gang are kept a secret.

4. *Raat ke dhaai baje:* The *B Gang* knows that all customers are always looking for more suppliers. And The *B Gang* works assiduously to eliminate competition. The more the number of suppliers, the lesser the quantum of business, and the more delayed the payments are. To ensure customer loyalty, the *B Gang* is always at their service. "*Aap ko koi bhi zarrorat ho mujhe call kijiyega (Call me if you need annnyything),*" is a common statement. "*Raat ke dhaai baje bhi (Even at 2:30 am).*" While *kaise hoga* causes negative association, this principle causes positive psychological association. Because the customer is dependent on the *B Gang* for so much more than just supplies, they get more orders and quicker payments.

We came up with our own modifications to these principles and Alok, from my team, is really good at these:

1. *Aap pe bharosa hai*: I like to call this the *burden of confidence.* When Alok sees that a customer's payment is about to be due, he calls them as a reminder. Not of the due date but of how confident he is that the customer will not delay the payment. He uses *just do it* and *kaise hoga* in advance to let the customer know how valuable they are, how much their orders mean to us, how well they have treated us in the past, and how grateful we are to be supplying to them.

This *burden of confidence* is enough for most customers to make the payments on time and, if not, call in advance to tell us that they are sorry for the delay of a few days.

This also creates a psychological association that has no negative value. It is *raat ke dhaai baje* without the extra effort.

2. *Raat me sote hain*: *Raat ke dhaai baje* has a nasty flipside. It reduces your weightage and people start taking you lightly. Also, favours start increasing in cost and time required until your full time job becomes appeasing customers. We didn't want to go down that route. So, we created the *raat me sote hain* principle. There are days when, at 9 pm, a customer starts calling frantically, and we choose not to respond till 9 am the next day. Because we don't take calls post 7 pm.

   We might have been in the office, working till 11 pm that day, but the customer thinks we'd retired for the day. Interestingly, it gives our customers the sense that we are a *professional* company. We have indicators of when this rule needs to be bypassed but more often than not, we aren't available outside office hours. And our customers take us more seriously because of this.

3. *Aapka order bana rahe hain:* Instead of invoking reciprocity through gifts, we invoke it through perceived future supplies. Each customer has an order cycle that we've studied over time. We call the customer telling them how we have already started producing material for the order we *know* they will give in some time. And because we have started work on that order, we would very much appreciate our previous bills to be cleared so that the next order can reach them in time.

This works well for both order acquisition and payment recovery. It's a combination of the *burden of confidence* and *reciprocity*. We convey our confidence in the customer by already having thought about them and preparing their next order. And by associating their next requirement to the due payment, push them to pay sooner. All this, mind you, is when we don't yet have an order from the customer. Sometimes, as a bonus, it helps us eliminate competition. Our customers frequently say, "I was going to give this order to another party but since you have already started working on it, I'll give it to you."

Overall, *takada* is an important skill for every small business to have in their team. Adding our own twist to it has allowed us to optimise payment recovery, while ensuring that we aren't taken lightly.

4

Mehngai dayain

On paying too much for cheap stuff

A poignantly lovely song from the movie *Peepli Live* goes:

> "Sakhi Saiyan Toh Khoob Hi Kamaat Hai
>   Mehngai Dayain Khaye Jaat Hai..
>   Pehle Tagde Tagde The
>   Ab Duble Patle Ho Gaye Saiyan"

High costs affect all businesses sooner or later. Sooner for small businesses. Small businesses are especially vulnerable to fluctuations in costs due to low margins. But small businesses are also vulnerable to spending exorbitantly on things that cost almost nothing.

Let's consider an example. Most small businesses invest in accounting software by Tally. The software is great but one license costs about Rs. 18,000. People invest in this software because their CA demands tally data and charges extra if you go to them with a piece of paper or an Excel sheet.

When I took over the company, our tally license had just expired. I was hounded by my accounts team to buy the new license. Except there's a better and more economical solution- Zoho. Zoho Books is an online accounting tool, much more user friendly and less costly than Tally. It also allows you to export your data in Excel and Tally data formats. The base version of Zoho, applicable to most small businesses, costs Rs. 2499 per year and provides access to 3 users. The best part is that if your business has an annual turnover of less than Rs. 1.5 Cr and has GST registration, you can use Zoho for free. There are many similar tools available online that can provide online accounting solutions for almost or at no cost.

Similarly, people spend way too much on getting a website built. I know, having a website is almost a necessity these days. Some people also want a mobile app. You might think that small businesses, especially small shops, wouldn't have the need for this. Think again. Most businesses need a fairly basic website and app, displaying details about their products and allowing users to contact them. A digital presence is a strong differentiator for small businesses.

Costs for websites range from Rs. 10,000 to Rs. 50,000 where I come from. And then there are maintenance charges. And fees for updates. It's a costly affair. But doesn't have to be, right? The techies are already scratching their heads reading this.

Enter Wix. And Weebly. And 123Sites. And GoDaddy. And a

multitude of other options for people to build websites at almost no cost. E.g. on Wix, one can create a website for free. The website name in such a case is of the format- *yoursite.wix.com*. If you wish to buy a custom domain (*yoursite.com*), you can do it on GoDaddy, then connect the Wix site to this domain using a Wix Premium plan. My Wix premium plan costs me Rs. 348 per annum. The domain I bought cost me Rs. 1300 per annum. Domains are available for as low as Rs. 200 per annum.

It took me about a week to get the website up and running. It works well and I have no complaints. Yes, the designers cringe. And the techies mock me. But they're not the reason I built the website. I built it for my customers to have a ready source of information. I built it for my sales agents to quickly share details about the company. It is for my sales team to flaunt on their visiting cards and quickly show a customer what we're about.

Could I have spent Rs. 20,000 on a *better* website? Maybe. Would it have generated additional value? Absolutely not. How do I know this? It didn't. For small businesses, websites are important to have. But don't generate many leads. The leads come from other marketing strategies- Amazon, door-to-door marketing, cold calls, etc. It took 6 months for our website to generate a positive lead. Was it important? Absolutely. Was it worth Rs. 20,000? Absolutely not.

Similarly, for mobile apps. Important to have. Not worth spending much on. We use Glide Apps. All you need to know about building an app using Glide is how to use Excel, or Google Sheets specifically. It took us five days to get our mobile app running. How much money did I spend? Zero. Our app is still under the free plan. I don't need to publish it on the Apple App Store or Google Play Store. I just share a link, you open it, it prompts you to save it to homescreen, and you can have my app on your phone.

Check out: loveprofitdhokha.com and lpdbook.glideapp.io. Pretty cool, right? Techies and designers, shut up.

All these expenses come under the *good to have* category. Everytime an expense crops up from this category, the automatic response should be:

1. This can be done for almost no cost
2. We can do it ourselves

Most of these *good to have* expenses tend to be software related. Even the *B Gang*, with all their prowess, is susceptible to this. That's not surprising because the level of digital literacy in India, by some estimates, is below 20%. This estimate, thankfully, is not solely based on people's ability to use WhatsApp and Facebook on their smartphones. And, let's face it, technology is intimidating. Flutter, Kotlin, Java, HTML, CSS, React- you wish these were names of cupcakes or cocktails instead of programming languages you need to know to develop websites and mobile apps. Having a techie friend doesn't help. They've used these names so many times with profound looks that you assume that building even a simple app would be a nightmare for a non-techie.

And me telling you about low-code or no-code tools isn't

helpful either. Because you believe that even those tools would have some secret sauce only quasi-techies (engineers without a software background) can understand. So, not that you couldn't do it, it would just take you so much longer. And you don't have the time.

I'd tell you how wrong you are. I'd push you to try it out and realize how simple it is. But you wouldn't have gotten to this paragraph if you were willing to do that. So, you need a saviour. Someone who can build it, teach you while doing so, and not cost much.

Enter the humble, high school student. Okay, maybe not so humble. High school students, in any case, are the most underutilized talent pool in the country. They are tech savvy, open to interesting projects, and love pocket money.

So, how do you find them? Go to an affordable private school with a decent reputation and a computer lab. The others aren't worth it. Don't assume the presence of a computer lab. Data shows that less than 27% of schools in India have access to computers.

Talk to the principal and tell them that you have an internship opportunity for their students of classes 8-12. Print a poster, stick it on their notice board, speak to the students during their morning assembly, and brief them about the project. Inform them about the low-cost tools they need to use for development. Finally, make it into a competition. The winner gets Rs. 3000 (or whatever sounds good enough) as a reward for the best project.

Shortlist 3 teams (of one or two students) based on some cooked up criteria (basically identify the nerds) that doesn't hurt the losing teams. Or maybe it does. That's how the world works, they should learn. Work with the teams over a couple of weeks to finalize the solution. Learn critical aspects on the way, such as how to keep updating your website on your own. Declare the winner at the morning assembly. Hand them the money and certificates (printed in your office). Get lost until you have another project.

You get your website or app. The nerds get recognition and some pocket money. Either or both give them enough joy to get them through the remaining years at school. The school gets marketing material to showcase their students' achievements.

Now, you have no excuse. Stop spending on stuff that should cost close to nothing!

5

Mere sawalon ka.. jawab do... do na

On culture within the company

My engineers ask me about current market dynamics, the sales team asks me about metallurgy, the security team asks me about sales strategy, and I love it. I've always loved being asked questions so it came naturally to have an open-door, transparent policy for questions.

People seek me out to have conversations about a whole host of subjects whether relevant to the company or not. This created many unexpected advantages. It helps us bond, know each other better, share our fears and insecurities, and have a laugh when our tiny world seems to not make sense.

I have read often that when it comes to culture in an organization, it's about '*monkey see monkey do*'. I was unpleasantly surprised, then, when a few times employees came to me complaining about someone from another department who was 'asking them about their work'. They took it as a hostile invasion. I spent quite some time talking to the team about proper ways of giving and asking for feedback. It only went so far. I found out that '*monkey see monkey do*' only works with ideas and processes that feel natural to people. When they encounter something unnatural, even if admirable,

Monkey see monkey no do!

This bothered me. I have read enough to know that working on culture within an organization is important and since open answerability was an important value for me, I wanted it to percolate in the team too. So, I made it compulsory. In a team meeting, I explicitly stated that

Everyone is answerable to everyone.

Stating it properly was important. The onus was not on people asking the questions but on those being questioned. Providing satisfactory answers was the latter's responsibility. Was there friction? Absolutely. It was utterly unnatural for someone from the maintenance team to answer to the sales team why a particular machine had malfunctioned. In turn, the sales team was very uncomfortable answering to the maintenance team about why we didn't have enough orders.

It still feels unnatural to people to answer but they make up for it by asking more questions. It's become a bit of a competition of who is asking more questions than having to answer. And I can live with that.

What I hadn't foreseen were some interesting advantages that came from doing this. There developed a sense of *shared answerability*. Since people knew more about each other's work, they would step in to answer for the other. In a tight situation, people were more comfortable offering and accepting suggestions and help. Nothing is more annoying than an enthusiastically helpful colleague offering suggestions on something they know nothing about. *Pata nahi hai toh bol mat (Don't offer suggestions when you don't know anything about this)* used to be a common comment flying around the office, antagonising many. Those comments reduced drastically.

It also brought some very selfish advantages to me. I love answering questions but not the same question too many times. Now, whenever that happens, I point the person to a colleague who I think can satisfactorily answer the question. It saves me time and frustration, while still allowing the person to get their answers.

The biggest advantage, though, was that a decentralized system of checks and balances emerged. All companies have hierarchical, centralized systems for reporting and monitoring. A few people are tasked with raising red flags and they're bound to miss something. In a small business, it's usually the CEO. I used to constantly be under pressure to ensure that all reporting was done properly and on time. Much of that was solved through steps discussed in Data Kitthe. But there would often be something that I or someone else missed. Now, I had a new weapon- everyone! People were asking each other for answers all the time. And the sneaky red flags became more visible.

Too many questions

Fellow entrepreneurs don't generally respond well to the above strategy. The common refrain is,

> "If they keep asking questions all the time, when will they do their work?"

It's not an unfounded concern, just short-sighted. Most entrepreneurs try this strategy but get too overwhelmed too soon by the flood of questions that has just been released. They imagine that this will always be the case. And the flood will keep coming, again and again.

Another popular refrain is,

> "They'll get stuck in *analysis paralysis.*"

Really? From having the freedom to ask questions? As Wolfgang Pauli, the theoretical physicist, liked to say, "That's not even wrong." So, I won't care to comment.

The truth is that the flood arose in the first place because until then, employees had no gateway to ask questions. Their questions were bottled up. Of course, when first allowed to do so, their questions would come pouring out. There's a *lot* they want to know. No matter how communicative you've been about the company's vision and strategy, they have questions, as they should.

It's difficult to translate a few sentences of vision and strategy into operational decisions on an hourly basis. Maybe not for you. You've overthought this. You've gone through every scenario and situation in your head. Which is great, but it's in your head.

For employees to act in alignment with the vision and strategy, they need operational support too. They need to be able to talk to you and each other about how to tackle a particular solution. As these questions come up, it also becomes much easier to automate generating answers.

Let me give you an example. Our vision was to become the most cost-effective supplier of our product in the country. What does that mean? For us, it means that we have different rates for customers in different geographies, while keeping in mind the local competition in that area. The question I had to field multiple times a day was, "What rate should we quote to X customer in Y region?"

The process of coming up with the answer was firstly to find out what were the prevailing rates that our competitor was offering in the region. Then, decide on a price to match or beat the competitor's offer. Coming up with the best price we could offer involved a calculation of two parameters:

- Average sales price: How the new price would affect the average sales price of the product.
- Average cost price: How much the increased volume would decrease (by economy of scale) the average cost price of producing the product.

This would also cause a lot of discussions (read arguments)

within the sales team about the best price to offer. Obviously, I was supposed to have the final answer. After doing the above calculation multiple times a day for many weeks, I hired a consultant to build a machine learning algorithm that would analyse historical data of the past few years and calculate the best price offer for us.

Haha, got you there!

I made a Google Sheet. The sheet, within 10 columns and 15 rows, gave us a quick way to calculate the above. I shared the sheet with my head of sales and the question now hardly comes up. I just spend time reviewing, a couple of times a week, whether the process is being followed properly and that our profit margins make sense.

Most of the repetitive questions can end up being resolved similarly through shared knowledge and tools. For the rest, take time out from your unnecessarily busy schedule to answer them.

6

Chor chor mausere bhai

On dealing with a thieving employee

If you think this isn't relevant to your company, you're wrong. In fact, you've probably already started thinking about *that* person. Maybe even started making a mental list of people. You know them in your gut. Every so often, you find something out that makes the silent voice inside you start screaming, "Get rid of them!"

Except you can't. They're too important to let go. They handle responsibilities well. They get work done. They're always willing to go that extra mile. The team depends on them. And they never disagree with you.

Wait, that's the catch. They *never* disagree with you. I've found this to be a good way of fishing out people who steal and cheat. You know the kind. Forever bent slightly forward as if ready to lie prostrate at your feet at any moment. Mostly soft-spoken. Saying *yes* three times to your every statement. Unconditionally complimenting you. Bending forward even lower with each statement as if getting ready to give you a piggyback. Trying to get ever closer to you like a lover trying to know your deepest secrets. They want to be your true confidantes. All in an attempt to steal more from under your nose.

Before we proceed further, let's outline a few principles:

1. *Har chaploos dhokha dega* (All sycophants are untrustworthy)
2. *Har chaploos chor nahi hota* (Not all sycophants are thieves)
3. *Saare chor chaploos hote hain* (All thieves are sycophants)

If you have one around you and you still have your head on your shoulders and feet on the ground, get serious about them. I say this because it's very likely that you're already under their spell. They've clouded your judgement to an extent where you would never be suspicious.

Let's be honest: All leaders are narcissists. At some level or another. And a sycophant knows this better than anyone else. Narcissism is fertile breeding ground for sycophancy.

When I had accepted my own narcissism and fallibility to sycophancy, it wasn't difficult identifying the thieves. Multimethod validation (discussed in the chapter 'Data Kitthe') also helped when I found it difficult to convince myself. It *is* difficult. You trust this person, they're good at their job, and stealing feels like a personal betrayal you don't want to accept. But the sooner you do it, the sooner we can get to action.

Now, let's be clear, we're talking about a specific kind. Not the dull ones. Not the ones who whither under a strong gaze. We're talking about the smooth foxes.

If you don't know who I am talking about, keep looking. If you know, you have my sympathy.

Within the first couple of months of taking charge of the company's operations, I identified that a senior member of my team fit the above criteria well. A little digging revealed that my doubts were indeed true. Now, it so was that this person (let's call him Mr. S) was the Head of Sales and Purchase at the company. That right there is a double whammy.

Mr. S had control over both money coming in and money going out. Before we get into how I dealt with this situation, let me just state what you already know: people who steal from the company are generally involved in sales, purchase, and/or accounting. If you've been as foolish as me to have put one person in charge of any two or more of those departments, please correct it; if this person is also a sycophant, we can meet and cry together. No words, just you and me (no holding hands).

Mr. S, as expected from such a situation, was stealing through every channel he could. He was involved in financial decision-making on three levels: negotiating and finalizing sales prices with customers, finalizing raw material prices with vendors, and arranging for transport for the finished product. He had created ties on all ends: he would convince customers that he should be paid a commission to convince the management (me) to lower the sales price; a similar commission from vendors to convince the management (me again) of a higher cost price; and a commission from transporters to play favourites and, of course, jack up the transportation price (I want to kill myself).

To deal with this, I first identified which was the largest source of his income among the three. It happened to be the second – from vendors of raw material. And I let that be majorly untouched. I would keep a tap on how much he was earning through this and step in when the amount seemed too hard to digest. What I did, though, was to get my most trusted colleague to start contacting vendors without ever discussing commercials. This was done under the pretense of expanding our vendor base.

On the sales end, my action was swift. I started talking to customers directly for price finalization. I also slowly increased the sales team from two to four, and started distributing clients among them.

The transportation end was the most tricky. Transporters aren't well organized and were mostly located in other towns. They would arrange for trucks remotely. I could never figure out how much he was earning through them and how to stop it except by removing him. I did one thing, though. I have a habit of sitting on the patio outside the factory every evening to get a chance to chat with workers as they leave for the day. I started using this time to also interact with truck drivers and give them the sense that they could reach me directly if they faced a problem.

And one day, it worked. A truck driver created a ruckus outside the factory, demanding to meet me. Arguments with truck drivers aren't uncommon around factories but are generally settled outside the office. This time, however, the driver insisted on meeting me. I got my opportunity. I called him into my office and he told me about how Mr. S had duped him of his money under the false commitment of getting him higher payment from the company. After some customary digging around, I let Mr. S go.

Dealing with the situation required:

- Strengthening the team (through principles from *Ghar Ki Murgi Daal Barabar*)
- Reducing people's (customers, vendors, transporters, and the rest of the team) dependence on him
- Keeping his income majorly unaffected until he was removed

I knew it would require the above when I came up with the strategy. What I didn't know was how much patience would be required too. It took me 11 excruciating months to finally reach a position where I could let him go without fearing that he could do irreparable damage. He tried - bad mouthed to customers, lied about quality problems with our product, started working with a competitor and diverted a few of our customers, and even went to the extent of spreading rumours that our company was on the verge of shutting down.

By then, though, the team was strong enough to deal with the situation. Within a couple of months, all the rumours died out. Quality concerns were alleviated as soon as customers received their next lot of material, diverted customers came back to us because our product was better, and no one who mattered believed that the company was going to shut down. A few months later, I got news that our competitor had also kicked Mr. S out – either because the customers he had diverted came back to us or because a thief is a thief anywhere they go.

The 11 months of keeping Mr. S around were full of other fears too. *Would my team lose faith in me because I wasn't taking perceivable action against a dishonest employee? Would Mr. S drive away people trying to fill his shoes? Would others succumb to his ways and start supporting him? Would his accomplices within and outside the company create problems? Would customers stop working with us? By keeping him around, was I letting him strengthen his hold further?*

All of the fears came true, one way or another. I have no way to know whether he could have been removed earlier and how the counterfactual would have played out. Could I have done more? Was I trying to play *too* safe? I won't know and it bothers me. But what gives me peace is that when, finally, the decision was taken, the team was ready to handle any repercussions that arose.

II

Grow

7

Lohe ke daane ka dhandha

On understanding your business

My friends don't know what a steel plant looks like. Maybe you don't either. And it's important to set the right context.

India was the world's second-largest producer of steel in the world in 2018, producing 106.5 million tons. That's 106500000000 kg. Yeah, crazy! Until you find out that China, in the same year, produced 928 million tons of steel (*head blows up*).

An important data point is that out of the total quantity of steel produced in the country, over 40% comes from SMEs. Manufacturing SMEs (small and medium enterprises) are companies with a total investment of less than Rs. 10 Crore in plant and machinery. There are 56 million SMEs (manufacturing and service-based) in India, which employ 60 million people and generate 1.3 million jobs per year. By an estimate, 95% of industrial units in India are SMEs.

Another thing to understand is that the large majority of these SMEs are dependent on large enterprises (those that account for the rest 60% of production). SMEs play the role of ancillaries or supporting companies, producing components and materials that are used by the large enterprises.

Our company is a small enterprise. We are mostly dependent on the automotive industry for the sale of our products. You might have started guessing what our condition would have been in recent times due to the deep plunge in the automotive sector. It wasn't nice. We'll get into that in Market Ki Maar.

There are various ways to categorize steel manufacturers- by size, product, etc. But the easiest way, for our purpose, is the credit cycle. All steel companies create products that sell in either of two ways:

- Nakad- instant payment i.e. payment is received before or right after the material is delivered.
- Udhaar- on credit of usually 30-90 days i.e. payment is received between 30-90 days after the material is delivered.

Now, we are part of an unlucky special category among SMEs- our raw material (steel scrap) is bought on *nakad* and our products are sold on *udhaar*. This translates to a much higher working capital requirement, constant tension of getting payment released from customers, and continual bickering with scrap suppliers for slight delays in making payments. You didn't think I was giving you so much background because I wanted to cry about it? It's not over yet.

Our final product also falls under the unfortunate category of 'industrial consumables'. These are materials that make up a small percentage of a company's requirement. Someone aptly described it as 'salt for the metalworking industry' – everyone needs it but no one needs too much. To help you understand: we have a production capacity of 1000 tons per month and a customer who buys 25 tons per month is a big customer for us. The average consumption of our product in industries is 3-5 tons per month. This means that we need a much larger base of customers than usual and all the worries from the previous paragraph get magnified.

Wait, we're not done. We produce small, spherical granules of steel (*lohe ka daana*). Our product comes in sizes ranging from 300 micron to 3 mm. The manufacturing process of our product is such that in one production cycle, we necessarily produce all sizes and then segregate them. Now, consumers always need one or two sizes of material. This means that we have to necessarily find separate consumers for every size we produce. If we don't, our stock keeps increasing which blocks the working capital. Also, if we find a new, big consumer that wants 20 tons of material, we need to increase production by 150-200 tons. And then find customers for the remaining quantity.

Our worries don't end there. But I'll stop my rant here. And because I don't want you to stop feeling sympathetic towards me yet, I'll discuss the flipside of such a situation in another chapter.

I spent so much time describing our business to tell you that it took me months to understand every aspect myself. And there is great value in understanding how your business, similar businesses, and the industry function. It is important to find out what pitfalls you'll have to face to grow your business. Understanding my business and the industry, inside out, was the first step towards growing and transforming the company. And most of it didn't come from Google.

There are two interesting aspects of the *loha* business I'd like to discuss: *kaccha kabadiwala* and *loha chori*.

Kaccha Kabaadiwala

Steel scrap is sold to SMEs majorly by small traders, demeaningly called *kabaadiwala* (junkman). Remember the person from your childhood, who used to come around regularly to pick up old clothes, newspapers, etc? These traders are the same except that they pick up and sell steel scrap.

The daily routine of such traders goes like this:

1. Wake up around 4 am
2. Get into the pickup truck they own or have rented
3. Travel to a location within a 100 km radius to pick up their first lot of scrap, usually between 2-5 tons
4. Bicker about prices, quality, weather, or anything else
5. Load the material on to the truck
6. Travel back to sell it to a bigger trader who has a stocking facility or manufacturers such as us

7. Bicker about prices, quality, weather, or anything else
8. Unload the material off the truck
9. Pay a bribe almost every time they cross a traffic police check post
10. Repeat steps 1-8 as many times and step 9 as few times as possible
11. Reach home by 10 pm

I know traders who do the above 4-5 times a day to earn enough to save less than Rs. 15000 per month. And they don't get any days off. They're a pain to deal with because they are unorganized, unregulated, and often loud and rowdy. But I have tremendous respect for their hard work.

Now, most of these traders also sell the material for cash. They don't have GST registrations, don't know how to make invoices , and some don't even have business bank accounts. This is called *kacche ka dhandha*- a business done only in cash without transactions through a bank account and without documentation (because of which they have to bribe the traffic police). Now, most of these traders don't earn enough to have to pay taxes. But the companies that buy from them, do. So, many companies buy this material in cash, use it to produce their product, and then sell it in *kaccha*. What that creates is a separate, untaxed source of income for these companies, that some call 'black money'.

Since we didn't want to do any of this, we pushed all our scrap suppliers to get GST registration. Our accountant helped them with the process and also taught them how to create invoices and file GST returns. This helped reduce their burden of bribes and also made them eligible for bank loans because increased bank transactions made them more credit-worthy.

I'll let you spend a moment or two commending our noble act.

Now, the utterly selfish reason for doing this. These small traders do the hard work and face all the harassment but couldn't sell directly to us. They didn't have the relevant registrations to give us an invoice. We don't purchase material in *kaccha* quite simply because we don't need to. Even if we wanted, we couldn't because all our customers buy in *pakka* (through bank transactions). What happened, then, is that these small traders would sell to big traders who could give us invoices for the material. The big traders charge us higher to earn a commission. Also, because there are fewer big traders, they would sometimes collude to drive up prices. So, by helping these *kaccha kabadiwalas* become registered traders, we were able to ensure that there was enough competition in the market to not cause an unfair increase in prices.

Told you, utterly selfish!

We learnt a couple of important things:

1. Never have complete dependence on a small set of suppliers
2. The greater the competition, the lower the price. If there isn't enough competition, create some.

Loha chori

Some of the most enjoyable (only in retrospect) aspects of running a business have been figuring out how people were duping us. In the case of steel scrap, it happens primarily in two ways– grading and quantity.

Grading is the process of identifying what quality of scrap has been supplied. The quality of scrap defines how much price will be paid for the material and is categorized into *heavy*, *commercial*, *light*, and *teena* (thin plates of steel, nothing to do with the metal tin). The trucks that bring the material rarely have only one kind. Different qualities of material are mixed together. The usual grading process would work so:

1. Material received
2. Loaded vehicle weighed
3. Material unloaded
4. Grading done
5. Unloaded vehicle weighed
6. Payment made according to relevant quantities of each category

'Grading done' is easier said than done. Once the material was unloaded, there was always an argument between my team and the supplier about how much of what type was present. Sometimes there would be bricks or other rubbish hidden below the scrap pile. Passing off some quantity of a lower quality material as higher quality meant more profit for the supplier and less usable material for us.

They would hardly ever come to a consensus and it would always reach me. And I could never be sure. How does one visually decide from a pile of mixed material exactly how much of which kind there was. I have heard legends of people who are supposedly really good at this. Not me. And I had no intention of competing with them. Sometimes, the argument would descend into, "Your staff doesn't even know which material is which kind. How will they ever decide?!" I would never have a satisfactory answer because, well, I didn't know either.

We solved this issue in two ways. Firstly, we stuck a board with pictures of different categories of material near the factory entrance. Our grading would be done according to those, no questions asked. Secondly, we made it a rule that traders had to organize different categories of material in different sections of the truck. And each type of material would be weighed separately. If a truck had material too unorganized to be unloaded quality-wise, it wouldn't be allowed entry. If the material was organized, there would be multiple rounds of weighing. This taught me to,

> *Always make your standards explicit without room for doubt*

The traders protested saying they couldn't wait for so long as they had more lots of material to pick up and loading quality-wise also takes too much time. We didn't budge. After a few times that trucks had to return from the factory because we didn't accept the material, they fell in line.

I heard another interesting story of *loha chori* but never experienced it first-hand. An experienced steel businessman told me that he's seen traders employ a cool trick for duping customers. Apparently, after loading the truck with scrap, suppliers sprayed rice water and then threw sand or dust over it. The dust would stick to the metal because of the rice water and increase the weight of the material. To give you a sense, steel scrap sells for between Rs. 20,000-25000 per ton. Every kilogram of dust passed off as steel during weighment would generate pure profit. I am still waiting for the day a supplier tries this with us.

Overall, the *kabadiwalas* are a fun lot to hang out with. Okay, fun may be an exaggeration. But they're definitely not boring. And that counts.

8

Ghar ki murgi daal barabar

As a leader, I fight two major impulses almost on a weekly basis, sometimes multiple times a day:

- They're not good enough
- Let me do it

Need to speak to a customer? Let me do it. Need to write a proposal for an Annual Rate Contract? They're not good enough. Need to negotiate prices with a vendor? They're not good enough *so* let me do it.

It's not difficult to find fellow entrepreneurs who think similarly. I would often meet an entrepreneur who'd be dissing their employees in front of me. Sometimes, purposefully when employees could listen. They thought it was a way to motivate the employees to do better. They couldn't have been more wrong. By openly declaring that they weren't good enough, the entrepreneur lost both the trust and respect of their employees. While I never suffered from this ailment, I did realize that I thought similarly.

I came to find that the above two impulses are slow poison in the process of building a team and infusing sustainability into a business. When thinking about this, for the longest time, I mixed up the above two impulses as inter-related. Each seemed to feed into the other and on evenings filled with frustration and burn-out, the potent combination in my head became, "They're not good enough so I *have* to do it."

They're not good enough

Actually, they are. They might not be great. But they very much are *good enough*. If never given an opportunity, however, how would any of them show you how good they are. In more cases than not, when I handed over an important task to someone on my team, they worked hard to complete it to the best of their ability. And it turned out *good enough*. It wasn't great. There was still work to be done. And that's where I needed to step in. Working with the team member on improving the output, in fact, ensured that the next time a similar task needed to be done, they were even closer to the expected outcome. The time I needed to spend on the task decreased every time it came up again.

I also realized my two major responsibilities as a leader: to coach and to support. *They're not good enough* is an impulse to shirk these responsibilities. Building a team is more than hiring the right people. The leader has to invest time and energy into growing the capabilities of each member of the team. Every team member should feel more confident regarding their work with each passing month. This requires the leader to give space to people to make mistakes, not be afraid to discuss them, and learn how to correct them. It requires the leader to coach their team on subtle nuances that they might be missing. And, finally, to support their team in growing their capabilities.

A great inspiration in this regard is Sridhar Vembu. He runs a company, Zoho Corporation, you might have never heard of. Started in 1996 as AdventNet Inc, Zoho currently has an estimated revenue of $500 mn, 3.5 lakh paid customers, and has been a profitable, bootstrapped company for 21 years. The most admirable aspect about this success is, in fact, Zoho's talent strategy. In the early days, as with any small business, they needed talented people but had neither the paying capacity nor the brand name to attract them. They focussed, instead, on *building* talent. Sourcing young not-graduates from rural areas around Chennai, they trained them in software development. *Coaching* and *supporting* these employees through on-the-job training and a clear linkage to employment (at Zoho), they created a supply chain of loyal, high-aspiration candidates. No question as to whether the strategy worked.

> **Finding talent** is *overrated*. **Building talent** is *over-looked*.

A good gym trainer never does your workout for you. They make sure you stay on track, that your form is correct, and are quick to help you if you make a mistake. When I started to look at my role from this perspective, delegating to and depending on my team became much easier.

I even took it a step further. Regularly, with no fixed frequency, I walk up to an employee and ask them what they've learnt in the past week or month. Initially, everyone would be taken aback by the question. It's not an easy question to answer by any means. Most of us spend years without ever asking ourselves this question. When I dig a little deeper, interesting stories come up- someone handled a pissed off customer in a novel way to keep from losing them, another was quick to take some action that averted a shutdown due to machine failure, yet another would share a learning from a family member that they have started applying at work. My learnings are so much richer because of these stories. And, occasionally, a story proves to me that they handled a situation way better than I would have.

I wouldn't have been *good enough*.

Let me do it

When I first started trusting my team with important tasks, it led me to a deeper issue- my misplaced sense of self importance.

This issue manifested in two commonly-heard statements:

- I work very hard
- I have no time

It also fed my workaholic nature. I was incessantly trying to impress upon people, especially those who didn't care or matter, that I *had* to work so hard because there was *so much* to be done and only I could do it. To cut myself some slack, initially there *was* a lot to be done that required my complete involvement. But before I knew it, I was filling my days with tasks that hardly required me anymore, only to keep feeding my wrongly derived sense of self importance.

When my team took charge of much that I used to do, I suddenly had time and didn't know what to do with it. And it dawned on me that the delay in practising trust on the team came from my fear of exactly this situation. Now, the same people (who didn't care or matter) I was trying to impress, would think that I was lazy, inept, or both.

This feeling might also have arisen from a kind of *imposter syndrome*. The feeling that if I wasn't working all the time and if people didn't think I was working *really* hard, they'd know that I am actually not the right person for this job.

The solution, that came after dealing with this fear, was to *relook* my role in the company and *find* ways to add value. I started spending much more time on strategy and innovation rather than operations, studied the market and industry extensively, worked on my (almost non-existent) finance skills. Suddenly, I didn't have the comfort of hiding in the shadow of unnecessary work. So, I worked hard to stay relevant to the company. This led to a breakthrough that helped us survive one of the worst recessions that the automotive industry (our primary customer) in India has faced.

I understood that as a leader, one should aim for increasing self-redundancy. There is *always* something more that can be done. But you can see that only when you're done with your current role. Pass on the baton, trust your team with it, coach and support them as they make you redundant, and then assume another role.

My 11th grade English teacher liked to say, "A good leader is like water - they take the shape of the vessel they're in." The role of the leader of a company *should* keep changing. If it isn't, the company isn't growing, nor becoming more sustainable.

But..

Oh, the but. There were times when I realized that the team really wasn't good enough. These were the same times when I realized I wasn't good enough either. There's a lot said about hiring people with complementary skills, ensuring a balanced team with the requisite skill set to execute all the relevant work for the company.

Really, who are we kidding? I don't have the money to hire the *right* people with *complementary* skills. Also, my business is in a small town where there isn't much in terms of local talent. And, as talented as you might think I am, I don't know everything. I know, hard to believe! But, sadly, it's true.

Now, the important thing to note here is that no one really likes learning new things. It's a painful process. Most of us came out of college swearing that we were never going to touch a textbook again. We got a job *so* that we would never have to study again. When people say that they're learning a lot in a job, what they basically mean is, "For the first time in my life, I am applying common sense to solve problems, while trying to justify my education by creating mostly unfounded connections with what I studied."

Everyone needs a strong incentive to learn something new. Until you were 15, you were too naive to know this. Towards the end of school, you started getting a *feeling*. By 2nd year of college you found out that all this learning was bullshit. But you were in too deep. So, you dragged yourself through the last years. And swore to never touch a textbook again.

Your team feels exactly the same way. And you either don't know enough or just don't have the time to patiently coach them on certain skills. So, incentivize learning.

We came up with a few simple ways of doing this. My team, on average, had a very low level of digital literacy. This created many problems, as you can imagine. The amount of work that went into creating a simple report was *just* crazy. To solve this, I offered my employees a deal. If they signed up for a course on computer training (at a local institute I'd spoken to), the company would bear 50% of the fees, offer them time off-work to attend classes, and give a slight salary raise to those who performed well in the course. For a couple of people, I made it compulsory to attend.

Another thing we started was monthly skill sharing sessions. Once a month, an employee would conduct a session with the team, explaining their work, the skills required and how to learn them, and tools they use to simplify their work. The person conducting the session enjoyed respect and admiration, which worked as a great incentive.

The efficiency gain from this has been remarkable. The team, as a whole, keeps growing their skills. And I keep being unpleasantly reminded of how little I actually know. There are a multitude of ways you can incentivize learning. Start with the simplest and focus on *building* the team. It's more than worth it.

9

Bhoos ke dher me rai ka daana

On dealing with Government officers

A fantastic song from Gangs of Wasseypur goes:

> "Bhoos ke dher me rai ka daana
>   Rang biranga bail sayana
>   Na milihe na milihe
>   Na milihe na"

In a nutshell, the lyricist is saying that it is futile to look for a mustard seed in a haystack or a colourful and smart buffalo. You won't find it.

These lyrics so well summarize my search for a sincere government officer that I could end the chapter here. But I can't let go of an opportunity to rant. 'Sincere government-officer' is an oxymoron. They don't exist. When they do, they're just exceptions that prove the rule (I'm not sure of the validity of that argument, just like how it sounds). Those of you screaming at me right now, you are or live with the exceptions. Happy?

Let me point out that this is not a question of honesty. That ship sailed a long time back. We all know what extraneous expenses need to be borne to get any relevant government-related work done. This is a question of whether the work will get done even after the expenses are taken care of. Here, unless you run a business that involves regularly interacting with the government, you'll need some clarification.

See, government corruption is a service that sells through two channels– B2C and B2B. The former is the experience you have when you go to get a driving license, birth certificate, etc. and, you know, give a 'gift' to the relevant officer for having graced you by their presence, and get your documents promptly. B2C is an efficient, hyperlocal form of corruption. You're the customer, you deal with one salesperson, their sales pitch (in hushed tones or signals) is clear, you pay the cost, get your reward. And remember to be grateful about it. You'll need to buy again from the same salesperson and you don't want them to hike their margin. I won't get into the cost of not giving a 'gift'. We all know it's not worth it.

Ghoos ka laddoo, khilao toh pachtao, na khilao to zaada pachtao

B2B corruption, on the other hand, is another beast altogether. Sales cycles are long, prices keep increasing from the moment the demand has been made, and you have to deal with multiple sales people (in increasing order of hierarchy). Once a payment has been made, you cannot know when, or if at all, the work will be done. For all you know, the officer gets transferred before the work gets completed. Then, the sales cycle restarts. Also, the B2B channel has a dynamic pricing policy. We'll discuss this shortly.

It's the perfect monopoly and the customer (you) is always on the losing side, like in a casino. Even when you win, the casino wins many times more. Combine the market penetration of Amazon with the margins of a casino and you get the corruption industry.

The insincerity in the B2C format is more easily manageable. You know whom to badger when your work hasn't been done. Insincerity in the B2B format is complicated because it's terribly difficult to know which link in the chain has your work held up.

So, I had to figure out how to get work done in this system. I learnt a few principles.

Frustiyao nahi moora, nervousao nahi moora

Another great song from the sequel to the movie, translated to,

> *Don't get frustrated, silly,*
> *Don't get nervous, silly.*

The first principle is to never let a government officer think that you're getting frustrated by how long things are taking because they'll just make you wait longer. The more frustrated you get, the more prices go up. Remember the dynamic pricing policy I mentioned? Well, this is one of the parameters based on which prices are escalated.

The second principle is to never show nervousness or fear. They can smell it, from across the desk, probably as soon as you enter their office. Fear is a great sales strategy. Have you come across those 'ionic bands' that are supposed generate or prevent (or whatever the hell they do) negative ions in your body? Completely unscientific, sells like hot cake. People are so afraid to have (or not have) these 'negative ions' in their body that they can't help themselves but buy one for every member of the family. Fear, in our case, is another parameter for dynamic pricing.

Let me narrate a hypothetical (*wink*) incident that happened with a *friend* (*double wink*) about a year after she took charge of her company. A team from a government department visited them for an audit. They were called beforehand to make hotel arrangements. They did. When this group arrived, they looked through every file and paper they could find, including those completely unrelated to their department. She thought everything was going great.

A day later, the head of the team came into her office with a subordinate. They spoke nicely. She was at her grateful best. After some chatting, the Head left, saying that he had to take a call. The subordinate told her that they had found some 'issues' in the documents and demanded Rs. 5 lakh to overlook it and create a positive report.

63

Yes, Rs. 5 lakh. She'd dealt with people before who demanded a few thousand and she had always complied (in fear and frustration). The number hit her like a brick in the face. There was no way they could have paid that much. She told them she'd think about it, unable to hide the fact that she might burst out crying at any moment. They left before she cried. That night, after speaking to multiple people who told her that she should just figure out a way of paying them (maybe in instalments?), she decided she wasn't going to do it.

She went back the next day and told them that there was no way they could pay that much, they were free to take whatever action they wanted to, and she was willing to fight a case in court. They stormed off after making a few threats. She spent sleepless nights. Until a few days later, when she received a call from the Head. In a jovial tone, he asked her, *"Aur Madam ji, sab kaisa hai (Madam ji, how are you)?"* After some banter, he proceeded with, *"Aap bataiye kitna denge (You tell me how much you can pay)?"*

Such conversations happened a few times and she kept saying that she couldn't pay anything. Finally, he met her again and settled for Rs. 30,000 to clear the 'issue' once and for all. When was the last time you negotiated and got a 94% discount?

That taught me something interesting. If you haven't read Rolf Dobelli's *The Art Of Thinking Clearly*, I strongly recommend that you do. It has taught me more about business than any other management book, except those by Peter Drucker and Clayton Christensen. In the book, Dobelli talks about the *anchoring bias*. This is a cognitive bias that greatly influences our thinking based on the first piece of information we receive. E.g. you walk into a local store to buy clothes. You like something and ask for the price. The salesperson quotes Rs. 1500. You negotiate hard, settle for Rs. 1200, and go home feeling very happy about the good deal. You don't know, however, that in more cases than not, the store still made a hefty profit on the sale. The discount had already been factored into the first price he quoted. He knew you would negotiate. But if he quoted Rs. 1000, you'd negotiate to maybe Rs. 900. He quotes higher so that you negotiate around that number.

What I learnt was the *counter anchoring* strategy. When quoted a price, you get back with an outrageously low price. Imagine if you started negotiating at Rs. 100 with that shopkeeper. If you shop regularly at Sarojini Market in Delhi, or similar ones in any city, you know exactly what I'm talking about. This is not an uncommon strategy. And once you state a price, you don't budge.

My *friend* used the same strategy. When the officer asked her how much she was willing to pay, she said Rs. 10,000. And, like I said, they settled for Rs. 30,000. This strategy only works when you know that the seller's costs are really low. In the case of a government officer, costs are almost zero. Anything over that is a profit. So, negotiate like a mad person.

> *Counter anchoring is the strategy to offer a ridiculously low price for a product or service you know couldn't have cost much to the seller.*

When you do so, you give the following signals to the officer:

65

1. You actually don't have the paying capacity.
2. You know the problem isn't as complicated as they're making it out to be

Believe in number 1 and research number 2. The internet has enough information on whatever issue you are facing. It's absolutely not as bad as they are making it out to be. Whatever you do, don't call your lawyer or CA as a first step (more on this in *Consultant ke chochle*). And don't be in a rush to make a decision, no matter how strong the pressure. We discuss the principle of *aaj kare so kal kar* in *Love, Profit aur Dhokha*.

This principle applies slightly differently with government officers. It's not that you should delay a decision. You should just delay it until terms are acceptable. The officers will use fear, intimidation, humiliation, just about anything to get you to pay up quickly. Don't. Remember the two signals you need to give to the officer and stick to your guns.

Let me tell you about a bonus strategy for dealing with government officers. I like to call it the *vo humko chihnte hain* trick. *Chihnna*, a Bihari term, means *to know*. But it takes *knowing* a step further and suggests some level of intimacy or liking. Everytime my *friend* gets to know that a government officer wants to meet, she looks up the names of high officials from their department. When she meets the government officer, she mentions in passing, "*vo humko chihnte hain (he knows me well).*"

But it's a hit-and-miss. Can't aim too high or they'll call her bluff. Can't select direct seniors for obvious reasons. It's a strategy that needs continual refinement. The rewards when it's a hit, though, are quite fascinating. They become quite a bit more receptive and lower their expectations. Some start quivering in their chairs and that's just hilarious. I'd suggest playing safe with this one, though. A miss could severely backfire.

Finally, as much as possible, try to meet them outside their office. If you have the leverage, call them over. If not, ask, "*Sir, shaam me free rahenge kya (Sir, will you be available in the evening)?*" Meeting them outside their office makes sense in multiple ways. They're more open to making their demands upfront so the negotiation can start right away. They are also less prone to *tehlana* (the art of keeping one waiting, discussed in *Consultant Ke Chochle*). They have a specific attitude when you try to meet them in their office, summed up very well by Aman:

"*12 baje tak late nahi, 2 baje ke baad bhet nahi*
  (Not late until 12 pm and not available after 2 pm)"

Try to bypass the *tehlana* and get to the negotiations. The sooner we get there, the sooner the work gets done.

10

Consultant Ke Chochle

On dealing with consultants

Unbiased advice is a myth.

Take your time. Let that settle in. Stop thinking about friends and family. We won't get into that; it's a touchy topic. I'll just say this: They are the most biased.

Now that that's out of the way, let's talk about consultants in our lives.

Have you ever met a lawyer who told you that a case was straight-forward?

Have you ever met a Chartered Accountant who seemed happy with your accounting?

Have you met a website designer who told you that your website was actually perfect for the current stage of business?

These are all consultants. Anyone in your life, who offers advice but has no liability in case of your failure (sounds like your friends?) is a consultant. They are majorly unaffected by the outcomes of following their advice.

Nicholas Nassim Taleb has written much about this breed, summed up well by his quote from *The Bed of Procrustes: Philosophical and Practical Aphorisms*:

> "A mathematician starts with a problem and creates a solution; a consultant starts by offering a "solution" and creates a problem."

The reason no consultant can offer unbiased advice is that if they did so, in more cases than not, they wouldn't be needed. Mark Twain famously said, and I paraphrase,

> "It is impossible to explain something to someone, whose salary depends on them not understanding it."

A consultant's salary depends on biased advice.

I mentioned in *Bhoos ke dher me rai ka daana* that you should never talk to your CA or lawyer as a first step towards solving an issue. Well, because their salary depends on it not being solved. Or not without them, to be specific. There have been times when going through my 'trusted' consultant cost me multiple times more than getting the work done directly.

Their advice will always come with a critical appendage that takes one of the following forms:

- *Let me talk to them. I'll take care of it.*
- *It's too complicated to explain.*
- *I'm here to rectify your mistakes.*

Oh, is that so? Then why wouldn't you help me just avoid them?- Why can't you simplify it for me, aren't you supposed to be an 'expert'? Why can't you tell me what to say? I can form words too, you know!

Dynamic pricing, based on fear and frustration, also applies to these consultants. Ever met one who completes critical tasks before time? The CA starts calling you 2 days before the deadline, reprimanding you for being so forgetful as to not look at the 10-page list of compliance deadlines they'd shared with you. And, you know, now that things have got so delayed, they'll have to work overtime to get it done in time, which costs more. Otherwise, penalties!

An important manifestation of this is *tehlana*- the art of making people wait. Most consultants know this really well. The longer you have to wait, the closer you get to the deadline, the more frustrated you get, the more you're willing to pay. A lot of times, I've heard a CA repeatedly say, "*Abhi toh bohot time hai, kyu pareshan ho rahe hain (Why are you in hurry when there's so much time left)?*"

Consultants are in the business of misery.

They earn by letting you know how miserable a state you are in. And drilling it into you that they're your saving grace. I think Gajendra Verma summed up this attitude in his poetic masterpiece, "*Isme tera ghata, mera kuch nahi jaata!*" His motivations might have been different, though. Jerome K. Jerome wrote in *Three Men In A Boat*,

> "I had walked into that reading-room a happy, healthy man. I crawled out a decrepit wreck."

That's how I feel every time I speak with a consultant.

I once called in a technical consultant to the factory for inspecting the health of our induction furnace. He spent 4 days, stayed at a hotel, worked hard with the team to assess the system, frequently chided them for not being regular with maintenance activities, grimaced as he looked through different parts and components, and finally sat in front of me to present a 6-page report. The summary of the report was that if we didn't overhaul some major systems immediately, there's a *strong* possibility that we'd have to completely replace the furnace within 4-5 months. How strong? He didn't say. How would it happen? In any of an umpteen number of ways, too technically complicated to explain.

What he didn't know was that I studied Mechanical Engineering and my father studied Metallurgical Engineering. We also don't like intimidation. So, we decided to do nothing beyond our routine activities. We decided to wait and watch. It's been 1.5 years. We're still waiting and watching, while the furnace has been hooting and whistling as it normally does.

Another time, we were trying to resolve a legal issue. In the matter of a week, I had spoken to 6 legal consultants. We, sadly, don't have a lawyer anywhere in the family. By the end of the week, I was utterly frustrated with conflicting opinions, when someone suggested reading about Company Law. I bought a couple of books on the subject (most legal books are available near the local court in town), devoured them over 2 weeks, fired 5 of the consultants, and proceeded with the one who knew what the hell he was talking about.

Through my experiences, I have found the following important aspects about consultants:

1. *All successful consultants are sweet-talkers*

   Why would you want an unsuccessful one anyway? Successful consultants know the right things to say to win your reassurance in them.

2. *Most consultants are gasbags*

   A *gasbag* is someone who talks a lot without much substance or content. Yes, like those friends of yours. Exactly like them. This also means that most consultants are indistinguishable. You never know which one is right. And seniority doesn't help much. They all, the *gasbags* and the *lesser gasbags* speak in *consultantese*- a language taught in dark rooms and alleys that can be found only if you already know where they are.

3. *Consultants say what you need to hear to pay more*

In this respect, consultants are more dangerous than sycophants. Sycophants say what you want to hear. They feed on narcissism. Consultants feed on greed and fear, sometimes simultaneously. *Want to know if the market for your product is growing?* Of course, it is! *Want to know how bad this legal issue is?* Well, it threatens the existence of your company.

Let me spend a little more time on the last one and allay some fears. CB Insights published a report on the top 20 reasons for startup failure. 'Legal Issues' was #17. And, surprise, no startup failed because their accounts were not maintained in the right format! SMEs are quite similar to startups and many of the same principles apply.

Also, no government *wants* to shut down companies! Besides the fact that it makes bad business sense, the political ramification would be disastrous. Secondly, no government officer wants your company to shut down. Why would they give up on recurring revenues? Whatever the issue, it is in the best interest of everyone to get it resolved.

When feeding on fear, consultants have an interesting tactic. They inflict you with what could be called the *graveyard bias.* It is the opposite of *survivorship bias* (Read Dobelli now! Okay, after reading this book). The survivorship bias states that because we are exposed to more success stories than failures, we overestimate our chances of success. By inflicting graveyard bias, a consultant makes you overestimate your chances of failure. If you proceed without them and their terms, of course.

73

This is done by giving detailed examples of what terrible fate became of an obscure yet once wildly successful company because they didn't do what the consultant is asking you to. And the businessperson ended up in jail. And all the assets were seized. And now kids roam around the barren company holding lizards as toys. You get the gist.

> *The graveyard bias is a tendency to overestimate chances of failure.*

So, is all hope lost? Yes. Well, definitely if you are looking for a *good* consultant. They went extinct in the 16th century. Lights out. Good night.

There is some hope, though, if you can settle for a *good enough* consultant. They're rare too, but alive. Here are some ways to identify them:

1. *They have fixed rates, for their services, that don't change depending on how close to the deadline you are.*

2. *They don't charge on a per man day or man hour basis. Stay away from dynamic pricing as much as possible.*

3. *They freely share information and data. They'll send you relevant literature on the issue at hand. They won't keep important registration credentials (such as for government filings) exclusively with themselves.*

4. *They don't charge you for every short call you make to them.*

5. *Their interests are aligned with yours.*

The last point is not so much to identify a *good enough* consultant as the *right* consultant. The *right* one is who wins big on your win and loses big from your loss. If you find one, bend over backwards to keep them.

Overall, consultants are a weird bunch. You're lucky if you have them as friends (really?). The rest of us are doomed and should stay away from them as much as possible.

11

Graahak Bhagwan Hota Hai

The customer is never right

"A customer is the most important visitor on our premises. He is not dependent on us. We are dependent on him. He is not an interruption on our work. He is the purpose of it. He is not an outsider of our business. He is part of it. We are not doing him a favour by serving him. He is doing us a favour by giving us an opportunity to do so." - Mahatma Gandhi

Dear Gandhiji, with all due respect, that's utter BS. The truth is that customers are vile, selfish creatures who never let me know what they are really thinking, always look at me with suspicion that I am cheating them, and never seem satisfied with my services.

The title for this chapter comes from another poster outside a small business:

"Graahak bhagwan hota hai aur Bhagwan ko hum udhaar de itni humaari aukaat nahi
    (The customer is like God and to believe that God would need products on credit is blasphemy)"

When I read this quote, it gave me so much relief that I could openly express the mistrust and apathy I have towards my customer's demands. It helped me come up with ways of dealing with them.

Firstly, I want you to remember two rules about the customer:

1. The customer is never right.
2. If the customer seems right, refer to rule 1.

Everything you've learnt about *serving* the customer is wrong. Customers came up with those. It's an elaborate ruse to propagate self-inflicted pressure on suppliers to sell products that keep getting better and cheaper. You know when the customer is happiest? When you give them the best available product in the market for free. Everything they say is in an attempt to push you further in this direction.

You have read a lot about constantly working towards more customer satisfaction or better customer experience. Then comes Jeff Bezos with his golden advice on customer *obsession*. All of these are important. Some indispensable. But they only work if you have a way of measuring these metrics without

77

actually believing the customer. When you speak to a customer directly, they are never satisfied. The product could always be better and cheaper.

So, you need to measure how good your product is without depending on direct customer feedback. There are three simple ways of doing so:

1. *Sales Growth*: No matter how dissatisfied *that* customer is with your product or service, if your sales are growing at a good rate, you are fine. Let me give you an example.

   We sell our products across the country. There was a particular customer based in Punjab who always had a complaint about our material. We worked extremely hard to satisfy him. Then he had a complaint about the transportation taking very long. We worked with all our transporters to optimize the logistics such that goods reached him 1 day earlier than usual. That's a big achievement with respect to road transport. Then he had a problem with packaging. Then, with how long it took to dispatch material. The list went on. And then he would repeat the loop.

   At one point, we realized that none of these complaints came up soon after delivery. They only came up when his payment was due and we would call him as a reminder. Every reminder call would be about hearing a long rant about how dissatisfied he was. Incidentally, no other customer in the region had these complaints. And our sales kept growing. So, one fine day, we just stopped believing him. Everytime he had a complaint, we listened, told him that we didn't believe him because no other customer had that complaint, asked him for proof, and the issue would get automatically resolved. Finally, we told the customer that we wouldn't sell to him on credit. If he wanted to buy our product, he would have to pay in advance. We've been at peace ever since.

2. *Quality Assessment*: To be able to speak to an annoying customer with confidence, you should have great confidence in the quality of your product. And any other metric important to your sales process. Besides tracking quality of final product, we monitor lead time (the period between order confirmation and dispatch), delivery period (dispatch to delivery), and delay from committed delivery date. Those metrics ensure that we have enough data to not be fooled by customers (I talk about *how to measure* in *Data Kitthe*).

   Quality problem? We've sent you the quality report of your material on email and WhatsApp. You can get independent testing (from those in our verified list) done and if the results don't match, we will enquire further. In the meantime, send us our payment.

3. *Set clear expectations*: It's important to clarify to the customer what they should expect for the money they are willing to shell out. When I first took over the company, we had a customer who would often taunt me about how the quality of our products wasn't as good as that of a foreign manufacturer. In my desire to appease them, I

would respond every time with meek promises of us trying to improve the quality. The problem was– we just couldn't have done it.

For the price at which we sold the material, this was the best available in the market. Customers looking for very high quality products weren't our target segment and were paying 30-50% extra for the better quality. The next time, this person called me, I politely asked him to give me an order at a 30% higher price and watch as I deliver the best quality material he has ever seen in his life. He never got back to me on that.

Setting clear expectations for the customer allows you more peace and breaks that endless cycle of *better price for lower cost.*

Before I conclude this chapter, I want to share one critical learning with you. It's called *'burn the fucking bridge.'* This one came from a quote by Bob Marley:

"The truth is, everyone is going to hurt you. You just got to find the ones worth suffering for."

Every customer is a pain. In all the wrong places. You just got to find the ones worth suffering for. More importantly, you need to let go of the ones not worth it. Don't worry too much about burning the bridge. I know it hurts. It's easier said than done. You're scared that they will find someone else. But it's good for both of you. Life goes on.

I am quite amused by the number of quotes by romantic authors and poets that apply to the seller-customer relationship.

The one below is attributed to Richard Bach:

> "If you love someone, set them free. If they come back they're yours; if they don't they never were."

Every customer worth keeping has come back to us because our product was good, our pricing was right, or because they were just so in love with us. None of those seemed so when we rejected their order. No customer is worth compromising on your values (read business principles) for.

If you need more inspiration on taking that final step and dealing with the break up, listen to James Bay croon:

> *"So come on, let it go*
> *Just let it be*
> *Why don't you be you*
> *And I'll be me*
> *Everything that's broke*
> *Leave it to the breeze*
> *Let the ashes fall*
> *Forget about me"*

And then, burn the fucking bridge. That's not to say you should stop talking to them. No reason you can't still be friends.

12

Love, Profit aur Dhokha

On partnerships

> *"Happy families are all alike; every unhappy family is unhappy in its own way."*

Leo Tolstoy's famous words from Anna Karenina apply quite similarly to partnerships.

> *"Happy partnerships are all alike; every unhappy partnership is unhappy in its own way."*

All happy partnerships are happy because

- The partners like working with and are loyal to each other
- The partnership is generating growing profits for both
- The risk of failure has been minimised

The list of why partnerships became ugly is as long as the list of unhappy partnerships. We know some of the common underlying reasons- underwhelming growth, greed, increased liabilities, dishonesty, family circumstances. This could be your co-founder, you, a sales agent, or another company you partnered with.

For sure, there are some factors too out of our control to plan for. Your spouse lost their job and the business isn't at a level where you can support your family. You had to quit. A truck carrying a consignment of your products met with an accident, causing you to lose a majority of your working capital. No bank came to the rescue. You get into a fight for survival with the instinct- "live to fight another day."

More often than not, though, things turn sour between partners when the partnership starts doing well and the partners each have conflicting thoughts on how the company should now be run. Interestingly, it is the lack of planning for success that causes more failures. People get quite surprised hearing the story. 'They were doing so well, God knows why they separated!" is a common refrain.

Well, one partner wanted a higher salary while the other wanted all profits to be reinvested in the company. Your sales agent wanted higher commission but you wanted to get a higher market share at the same level of commission. Success dooms most partnerships.

Inevitably, the conflict feels like a betrayal. *How can they not understand what I am trying to say? Can't they see how wrong they are? How can we give up on such a great opportunity?*

I don't have much experience with co-founders but I do have enough experience with partnerships to have come up with the following rules:

1. *The jingalala plan*: From the Tata Sky ads, "*Isko laga dala toh life jingalala.*" Every partnership is meant to make life *jingalala*. So, I plan for it. I lay out a visibility for my partner and myself of what happens if life becomes *jingalala*. For sales agents, I lay out the commission I will be willing to pay at different sales volumes. This gives them a sense of what volume to aim for to be able to earn more. If it works for them, great. If it doesn't, it never would have.

   With potential business partners, I share a vision of where I see the company in the next 24 months, with and without the partnership. If the goal for the partnership makes sense, we work together. If not, no *jingalala*.

2. *Manage expectations*: The *jingalala* plan is great but can cause heartburn if results are underwhelming. My plans, though mentioning the rainbow we wish to touch, initially tend to be focused on results that I would have achieved even without the partnership. It's a way of quickly testing the waters before going all in.

   E.g. I hope to increase sales by 15% over the next 3 months without the partnership. That's what I set as the forecast for my business development partner. If, after 3 months the forecast is not or just met, no one has heartburn and I know the partnership isn't working. If the forecast is exceeded, everyone is happy and the partnership continues.

3. *Fuck intentions, know self-interest*: I have read and heard so much about *how to know someone's true intentions* or *how I never realised their true intentions*. Getting to know someone's intentions is a rabbit hole I spend no time tumbling into. I don't care what someone's intentions are, I only care about their self-interest. And if it matches mine.

The thing about self-interest is that it's easy to gauge. You know that the other person wants to make a lot of money. How do you know? You ask. *How much money do you want to make? How much sales volume do you want to achieve? How many customers do you want to reach?* Focusing on self-interest makes the questions more specific and asking easier. Even with potential employees, I promptly ask, "How much money do you want to be making in 12 months?"

I then lay out my self-interest. *I want us to make X amount of money, I want us to have Y% market share, I want us to get these customers.* Another way to look at this is to share a very specific vision for the partnership, one unadulterated by intentions.

This also allows us to clearly measure how successful the partnership has been. We were supposed to have Y% of market share and we didn't. So, we either work harder or say goodbye. There's no fuzzy talk around how one intended to achieve a goal. All that's important is whether the work done till date affords another chance at the partnership.

4. *Get the paperwork done* - Just trust me on this. Before you decide to work together, put all the terms on a document and get it legally registered. You can thank me later. Anyone who doesn't want to do this, isn't worth thinking of a partnership with.

   For this, and only for this, run first to your lawyer and CA. Accept all the sad bullshit they're going to ram down your throat about failed partnerships. Let them come up with a clear agreement document. READ IT. Word by word. Don't make any changes until you've discussed all terms with your potential partner. Have the uncomfortable conversation. And make modifications that feel fair to all parties.

The above rules also make sure that I am on my toes, not getting complacent about having a partner. I know that I am accountable because I have clearly shared my self-interests. If a sales agent reached their targets but I am not in a position to pay them a higher commission, I messed up. If an employee achieved their targets but I can't give them the raise I promised, I failed.

Too many people hide under the garb of good intentions. *I really wanted to but..* As the CEO, I am most gullible to this. It's easiest for me to make an excuse. I love Maya Angelou's quote on the subject,

> "Remember, people will judge you by your actions not your intentions. You may have a heart of gold but so does a hard-boiled egg."

I try to hold myself and everyone I work with accountable to this principle.

But you know all this. You know how difficult it is to assess intentions. You know that interests need to be aligned. You know that any partnership should be preceded with a clear strategy, business plan, pub crawls, the whole jazz. Yes, yes, you'll be more cautious. But you've always known these things. You still overlooked everything that *one time* and got screwed.

So, what was different about that one time? Well, *you* were greedy. You couldn't escape the allure of a seemingly once-in-a-lifetime opportunity. And the thing with opportunities is that they come attached with FOMO (fear of missing out). We've all heard that opportunity knocks on the door only once, and ever so lightly. And you'd had your ears stuck to the door for so long. How could you have let go?

So, let's clarify a couple of things about opportunities:

1. *There's always another* - Bill Gross, the founder of IdeaLab (a business incubator based out of California) has an interesting take on this. Idealab, in their words, "has incubated and participated in over 150 companies in a variety of sectors such as consumer internet and mobile,

cleantech, education, automation/robotics, blockchain, enterprise software, and networking." So, Gross knows a little more than usual about why companies fail and he gave Ted Talk on the subject. His insight:

The single most important factor determining the success or failure of a company was timing. Specifically, being *too early* to the party. Facebook wasn't the first social network, Microsoft wasn't the first computer software company, WhatsApp wasn't the first messaging service, Amazon by no means the first e-commerce site. Reliance wasn't the first company in textiles, oil & gas, or telecom. If there's a poster child of being late to the party (and then taking over), it's Apple.

The first desktop computer, Programma 101, was launched in 1964. The first portable computer, IBM 5100, in 1975. The Apple 1 was released in 1976. Portable media players had been around since 1983 (even earlier, by some accounts); the iPod was launched in 2001. The first handheld mobile phone was developed by Motorola in 1973; the iPhone was launched in 2007. Need I say more?

The most successful companies aren't those who have first mover advantage. They are the ones who have the *fast* mover advantage i.e. spectacular execution on multiple fronts. So, don't worry about FOMO. Worry about execution.

2. *No opportunity is worth it* – And by 'it', I mean the heartache of a failed-too-soon partnership or, worse still, a lifetime

of bickering. Most partnerships break up anyway. Read about the history of any of the companies mentioned above.

3. *Every relationship has a time-stamp*: Yes, my girlfriend said that to me once. It's good to acknowledge that if *happily ever after* exists, it's a rare species. There's an extremely high probability that your partnership does not fall in that category. Just being aware of this helps relieve the pressure of high expectations from one another.

4. *Aaj kare so kal kar* - There's a good reason why business incubators ask for how long the founders have known each other and in what capacity. You might have just met and *partnership cupid* might have struck. You're just going to get over the infatuation (even sooner if you decided to work together). Knowing someone and working with them are two extremely different things.

I once had the privilege of listening to VS Sudhakar, the co-founder of Big Basket. It was quite relieving when he said that his first venture was in partnership with four other individuals, who weren't friends (in the traditional sense) with each other. They hardly ever met socially, hardly knew each other's families, just worked really well together. A few of them got together to start Big Basket after a successful exit from the previous venture. It broke the myth of 'you need to partner with your best friend' for me.

When thinking of formally partnering with someone,

the longer you can wait, the more you can work with them on smaller projects, the better your chance of identifying whether you'd be good as business partners.

You'll get an opportunity again. But you won't get back the years you spent in anger and pain.

13

Chota Business

On the special powers of running a small business

If you run a small business, don't let anyone fool you into thinking that you're important. You're not.

Banks don't care about you. The government wishes you didn't exist. In fact, no one notices you as long as you're a small business. And no one will miss you if you're gone.

Believe it or not, this gives you special powers. And, for life's sake, understand that this is not a bid to empower small businesses. That won't happen. Not through a lame book, anyway. This is about certain sneaky advantages of being a small business that you can use to your benefit. Those advantages are *anonymity* and *desperation*.

Sounds ironic? It is. No one knows or cares about you, and you are *always* desperate. Before we move on, accept this. Do it. Do it now.

Anonymity is a special power because this means that you can actually be anyone. Any one of 56 million fellow SMEs.

Desperation has advantages because it allows you to get work done for much cheaper than if people associate you with a large business.

Let me give you another hypothetical (*wink*) example of my *friend* (*double wink*).

He once had to get a set of documents attested by a senior official in the civil court. Now, the *rule* is that for any documents to be attested, all relevant parties must be present in court with their identity proofs. Here was the catch. The relevant parties live in another city. Them coming to his or he going to theirs was a costly and time-taking affair neither could afford. They'd already gone through the process of sending the physical document to each person and getting their signatures.

Now, let me tell you what this person's office looked like (as explained to me by my *friend*, of course). It was quintessentially drab. Located on the second floor of a five-storey fancy-from-the-outside-yuck-from-the-inside building, the ratio of officers to civilians was 1:200 by his estimate. My *friend* stood outside gauging the situation. There were a few advocates outside the office. Every person who went in with a request was shouted at, humiliated, had papers thrown at their faces, and asked to meet one of the advocates who would actually get the work done. Bypassing the official was not an option as it would undermine his authority. The advocates stood outside like pets waiting for their master to throw bones.

And then, in a quick moment of acting preparation that would give Naseeruddin Shah the sweats, my *friend* breathed life into the role of the *chota vyapari*.

The key characteristics of the *chota vyapari* are old clothes, inexpensive smartphone, finds it too hard to smile, quick to bow down with their hands folded in a *namaste*, too tired to speak up but too troubled to shut up, and a victim of the 'system'.

As a person running a small business, the above shouldn't be difficult to emulate. That my *friend* always looks like he's been sleeping under a railway bridge crossing over a sewage canal adds a unique charm to the role. What can I say? He's just that good.

So, he went into the office to get shouted at. He knew this was a necessary rite of passage and wanted to get it over with as soon as possible to move on to the advocate who would actually get the work done. The conversation went like this:

> *Friend:* Namaste sir. Bahut dikkat me hain sir. Bahut ummeed ke saath aaye hain aapke paas. (Namaste Sir. I am in a lot of trouble, Sir. I have come to you with a lot of hope.)

> *Official:* Itna boliye mat. Kaam kya hai bataiye. (Don't

93

talk so much. Tell me what work you have.)

Friend: Sir, kuch samajh me nahi aa raha hai sir. Kya karna hai sir. Chota vyapari ko sab pareshan karta hai sir. Bahut pareshan hain sir.

(Sir, I can't understand anything Sir. What should I do Sir? Everyone trouble the small business person Sir. I am very troubled Sir.)

O: (visibly irritated but secretly happy on finding another prey) Arey bataiye na kya kaam hai! (Just tell me what the work is!)

F: Sir ye kagaz hai sir. Bola hai aapse sign karvane sir. Samajh me nahi aa raha hai sir. Dukaan band kar ke aaye hain sir. Aaj ka kamai bhi nahi milega. Baccha log ko kya khilaenge, aap hi bataiye sir. Upar se bolta hai tees hazaar ka fine lagega sir. Kahan se denge sir. Aap hi kuch madad kijiye sir.

(Sir, this is the paper Sir. They have told me to get it signed by you Sir. I don't understand Sir. I closed my shop today Sir. Won't earn any income today. How will I feed my kids, you tell me sir. On top of that, they said I will have to pay a fine of Rs. 30,000 Sir. From where will I bring the money, Sir. Please help me, Sir.)

O: (getting close to throwing the papers away, exactly where my friend wanted him) Tum chup rahoge ki nahi?! Paper padhne do! (Will you shut up or not?! Let me the read the document!)

F: Maaf kar dijiye sir. Aap hi bataiye kaise karna hai sir. (I am sorry Sir. You only tell me what to do Sir.)

O: (starts to read the document, exactly what my friend doesn't want him to do)

F: Sir kuch samajh me nahi aa raha hai sir. Chaar din se ghoom rahe hain sir. Koi nahi madad karta hai sir.
    (Sir I don't understand anything Sir. I have been roaming around this place for four days Sir. No one helps Sir.)

O: (Throwing the papers on the floor) Hum nahi karenge! Jao advocate se milo!
    (I won't do it! Go meet the advocate!)

Step 1 accomplished!

Now, the advocate was a woman. Replace 'sir' with 'madam' in the above conversation, put it on loop so that it goes on for 90 minutes, and up every behaviour a few notches to imagine what happened with her. By the end, the paper was signed and stamped with two of the three parties missing. Not only this, because my *friend* continued this act in front of her fellow advocates, she also put a special stamp on the paper saying that she had personally witnessed each party signing the documents.

I don't care if you think he's a fraud. He is a *chota vyapari*, who no one knows or cares about. But everyone knows that the *chota vyapari* has a difficult life and is always desperate. It's also important to state that most policies and laws are tilted against small businesses. The *chota vyapari* wants to stay as far from legal issues as possible while large enterprises have swathes of lawyers handling everything. Small businesses most bear the brunt of 'corrective' policies made to combat the mischievous ingenuity of large companies. If you want any proof, study the effects of the Nirav Modi scandal on access to credit for small businesses.

Anyway, the best part of my *friend's* solution was that he'd spoken to a consultant (yeah, they are everywhere like cock-roaches!) about getting this work done. They had quoted a price of Rs. 15000 for the entire affair. My *friend* got it done for Rs. 200. If that doesn't convince you of your special power of *anonymity* and *desperation*, nothing will. Stay miserable!

Bonus tip: If you're a man, find a male official to speak to. If you're a woman, find a male official to speak to.

You obviously are the best judge of which way to turn the dial on *anonymity* and *desperation*. In the *vo humko chihnte hain* principle, mentioned in *Bhoos Ke Dher Me*, we dial down desperation to almost zero. In the above example, desperation was quite high as you might have noticed.

Embrace the *chota vyapari* inside you. And go conquer the world! Actually, don't aim that high. Just fool a few people. And when you're done, spend some time thinking about how difficult life is for the actual *chota vyapaari*, whose role you played.

Haathi ke daat

In the early days of Oracle, much to the confusion of his handful of team members, Larry Elison would always describe themselves as a '15-member team' to potential customers. This wouldn't surprise the *B Gang*, although it would be hard to imagine them taking a software company seriously.

The *B Gang* and all good business people know the value of perception and appearances. To grow, you need to build confidence in others to trust you. No one has the time to assess your capabilities before giving you an order. They go by heuristics (rules of thumb) to make a rough assessment. Unfortunately, an important thumb-rule for customers is how many people work in the company. Giving them that appearance helps ensure that you are not shown a polite red light.

People have told me that this shows low self-esteem. That I don't believe my team can pull off an order by telling the *truth*. I believe it's the opposite. I completely trust my team to get and execute an order remarkably well, which is why I don't want anyone to think that we are less capable than a company with 15 employees. Also, if we do get the order and realize that we are short-staffed, we can hire more people.

The *B Gang* takes this principle further. Many of them are big businesses in the guise of small businesses. One of the *B Gang* members' companies has an annual turnover of over Rs. 200 Cr. He wears a *khadi* safari suit, travels in a Maruti Brezza, has an office of 500 sq. ft., and employs 4 permanent staff. He is a trader and has a warehouse spread over 2.5 acres, employing more than 150 workers. Counterintuitive? By design. He knows the advantages of being a *chota vyapari.*

So how many people does this company employ? 4 or 150? Depends on who is asking. A potential customer? 250. A government officer looking for 'gifts'? 4. He knows that a higher number increases expectations and perceptions of capability. A lower number, on the other hand, reduces expectations and perceptions of capability. He uses what works.

He enjoys a revenue per employee of over 1 Cr. And that's a great metric, which comes primarily from *lean business* principles. He only spends money on assets that increase revenue. Everything else is a cost that needs to be minimised. He pays 4 employees above industry-standards rather than keeping 10 employees, paid at or lower than industry standards, and constantly worrying about them leaving.

Can he afford a Mercedes Benz? Can he afford a 5000 sq. ft. office? Of course, he can. But it's never a question of affordability. It's a question of value. Do any of those assets allow him to generate higher revenues? If not, they're not worth the value.

Doesn't a small office create a bad impression on potential customers? Yes, so he arranges the best hotel rooms in the city. Whatever the negative perception be from the small office; it is more than made up for by the great hospitality. What about when he has to send a car to pick his customer up from the airport or railway station? He rents a swanky one for a few days.

Why invest in an asset for a whole year when it generates value only for a few days a month?

This principle is followed by some of the richest people in the world. They live way below their means and their companies are very frugal when spending on anything that doesn't generate value. Warren Buffet, Bill Gates, Mark Zuckerberg, the list goes on. The $10 desks at Amazon are legendary.

Perception is important but only when it generates value - in savings or revenue. We're a small company, so we can't give you a big 'gift'. We're a big enough company to execute that order.

The principles of *chota vyapari*, *haathi ke daat* and *lean business* have helped us tremendously. We have the smallest sales team among all of our competitors, while being one of the top three manufacturers in the country. We supply our product to some of the most reputed consumers in the country. Our factory is also operated over the smallest area, reducing the cost of land and manpower. We're currently the most cost-effective manufacturer of our product in the country.

Don't tell our customers!

III

Transform

14

Tum mujhe khoon do

On building loyalty

Any company takeover is messy. The messiest part probably being how the existing employees are going to react to the new management. When I started at the company, I brought in a few people who had already worked with me earlier. The large majority of employees, however, were from before we came in.

Among those from the old team, there had arisen two clear camps. One that welcomed us as the new management, the other that wasn't happy about the change. In the first few weeks, a funny story reached me in hush tones. Apparently there had been an open bet among employees on how long it would take for me to run away. The words, if I remember them correctly were, *vilayat me padha launda dhul dhakkad me kitne din tikega (How long with the foreign-returned kid survive in the dust and heat)*. The bet went from 15 days vs 30 days to 2 months vs 3 months before slowly dying out. Honestly, I wouldn't have put money on me. So I didn't expect a commission from those who won.

Another problem to tackle was the fact that people from the previous management were now part of a competing company. For the first few months, I would often get reports of important news about our company being leaked to the old management. Since they were now competing against us, this information would affect me deeply. I kept thinking for months about what they would use against us. Until, one day, I decided it didn't matter. I think I had reached the limit of my frustration when I told those close to me that I never wanted to hear about what people from the old management were doing, who was informing them of what, and what their plans were. I only wanted to focus on fixing the company and any time spent on not doing that was worthless to me.

Although I took this step as an attempt of self-preservation, it also conveyed confidence. In a few weeks, I realized that those sharing 'secrets' with the old management weren't interested in doing so anymore. Those informing me about them knew I didn't care. And that taught me my first lesson in building loyalty:

People follow confident leaders.

And one way to convey confidence is to *create shocking rules*, as mentioned by Ben Horowitz in his stellar book- What You Do Is Who You Are. People were strangely shocked when they realized I was genuinely not interested in gossip and that it wasn't welcome in any conversation.

But making a team out of this group of people required more than displaying confidence. And I felt that most people had lost loyalty towards the company. They had stopped believing that the management cared about them. The response towards me wasn't because they had anything against me personally. They had built apathy towards anyone in the management.

I would sometimes hear, *"Maalik aakhir maalik hota hai. Worker ko hamesha saamaan samajhta hai (The owner and management always treat employees like disposable items)."* The first step in rectifying this was making sure that health and safety was taken care of. I remember, in the first week, there was an incident where a labourer got minor burns on his leg. I was in the habit of taking a round of the factory every half an hour or so. When I got out of my office, I saw him sitting in the security room looking out helplessly.

When I reached and saw his condition, I immediately asked for ointment. All the first aid boxes had been removed by the old management because, apparently, 'people stole medicines'. After getting Burnol from my office and applying it on his legs, I asked someone to take the labourer to the local hospital for a check-up. I also sent someone to get boxes of first aid and put it in different places in the factory. When the Head of Security protested that they'd get stolen, I remarked that as soon as it got stolen, I should be informed. I would replace it without questions and anyone who wanted to take the first aid kit home was free to do so.

Somehow, none of those kits ever got lost. If any medicines were ever taken without information, no one thought it necessary to inform me. After this incident, we took active steps for health and safety including compulsory wearing of personal protective equipment. There were times when workers resisted. But every time someone had a near miss from an accident, people became more conscious of their own safety.

These small, inexpensive steps ensured that people felt cared for. It is not uncommon to find people working in utterly precarious conditions in small manufacturing units. That the management cared became a differentiator for us. This led to the second lesson:

Caring is a competitive advantage when building loyalty.

Because we cared deeply about everyone, they were much less interested in engaging with our competitors.

This was only the beginning, though. There were many steps to be taken but what mattered most was a shift in perspective. I once had the pleasure of interacting with Vineet Nayar, the former CEO of HCL Technologies and author of 'Employees First, Customers Second'. I found his perspective very helpful and came up with my own version:

Team over everyone else.

The first step in this direction was to ensure that no one could demean my team members around me. This included customers, vendors, consultants, mentors, or other team members.

Customers, in the early days, would often complain about my team not responding properly or in a timely manner, or that they had messed up an order. Then the team would start bickering among themselves about whose fault it was. The customers weren't wrong. But in every such situation, I'd call the relevant people to my office, put the customer on speaker, and take complete responsibility for the issue. After the call, I spent time with the team telling them that it wasn't fair for them to have put me in this situation and if there was a genuine problem, it should have reached me before creating a bad experience for the customer.

Slowly, we were able to move to a situation where such calls became rare. Today, in most situations, my team tells me in advance that a particular customer might call me with a grievance. They list out the steps they have already initiated to resolve the issue. I still take the call in the same manner as before. A post-call session with the team, however, is hardly ever required. That I would take the fall for them gave them the space to make mistakes and know that I would help them correct those.

A good team is bound by loyalty towards each other and the company. And building a team is a daily activity. It definitely does not stop at 'hiring the right people'. As a leader, it has been my ongoing responsibility to invest time and energy into the growth of the team, in and out of work. It is the daily task I take most seriously. Everything else can wait till tomorrow.

15

Tussi ja re ho..tussi na jao

On dealing with employees leaving

Employees fall under three brackets- *replaceables*, *ummms*, and *indispensables*. The *indispensables* are the ones I invest a lot of energy in. They are the ones who find purpose in working for and growing with the company. The *ummms*..well...ummm. The *indispensables* take care of the *replaceables*. The acid test for who falls in which bracket is what I feel like when they leave.

With the *replaceables*, it's pretty straightforward. Smile, goodbye, move on. With the *ummms*..well..ummm. *The indispensables* leave a hole in my heart when they leave. Not only because they're hardworking, smart, and passionate. But also because they start feeling like family. They make up the core team.

The first time an *indispensable* decided to leave, I was heartbroken. I felt rejected. I wanted to never feel that again.

I wrongly thought that the solution was to make sure that everyone was always happy. That no one should ever want to leave. When the second person left despite my best efforts, I was back to feeling the deep sense of rejection as earlier.

What made me feel better was accepting the fact that everyone thinks about leaving sometime or another. And most will, some day or another. It came from the realization that I had wanted to quit so many times. In fact, no one would have thought of quitting as much as I had. I was neck deep in shit, completely out of my depth, and constantly pretending that I had everything under control. I'd had thoughts of getting on a train and disappearing. How, then, could I expect someone else, with much lesser to gain or lose, to continue forever without ever thinking of quitting.

All employees will leave, someday or another.

Instead of getting consumed by this fatalism, though, I started looking for ways to minimize the possibility of *indispensables* quitting. And inspiration struck when listening to Million Reasons by Lady Gaga. Judge me all you want; it worked. The lyrics, as most of you might secretly know, go:

"I've got a hundred million reasons to walk away
But baby, I just need one good one to stay"

I needed *indispensables* to have *one good reason to stay*. All steps discussed in *Tum Mujhe Khoon Do* helped. But I think what helped most was them feeling like they were contributing to a shared vision. Our vision is to become the top manufacturer of our product in India by 2022. As of this writing, we are among the top three. Every success has been a reinforcing step in the direction of achieving this vision. Every failure was treated as a roadblock that needs to be overcome. And everyday, we head home knowing that there's still work to be done.

Sharing this vision and working with *indispensables* to help them realize how each of their efforts is contributing towards achieving this vision has been the strongest binding factor for the team. There is enough and more written about the importance of a shared vision and purpose. But what I needed to learn was *how to communicate this*.

This becomes most relevant when an *indispensable* feels like a failure. We've all gone through it, put in great effort into something, and seen it slip away. A good lead stops responding, sales targets are missed, a machine breaks down when we're trying to push for higher production, a truck meets with an accident leading to loss of material and the customer cancels the order because they can't wait, an employee falls sick on the day that they were organizing an important inspection, the list goes on and on.

Indispensables always take these failures personally, irrespective of whether it was their fault or not, whether things were in their control or not. When people feel connected to a vision, small mistakes can have big effects on their self esteem. They might feel that they aren't capable of executing the vision.

In such times, it became my responsibility to be the calm optimist. To let them know that it's okay to have made a mistake.

It's okay to accept that, sometimes, shit just happens despite your best preparations. It was important to work with them to figure out exactly which link in the chain failed. And how that link could be strengthened. They had to know that I wasn't disappointed. I also realized that no one needs to be made to feel worse about having made a mistake. They're already beating themselves down. They need to know that there is a way to fix it and I'm there to help them do it. I learnt that:

Sharing a vision is a continuous exercise in dealing with failure as a team

As soon as a vision is uttered, *indispensables* feel a burden to execute. They want to make sure they contribute towards it and get it absolutely right. Being there for them when they fail, as they will, and as I do more often than any of them, gave them the reassurance they could pick themselves back up and grow stronger. I can take care of the rest.

I believe that this is the *one good one to stay.*

Actually, there's one more. Sorry, Lady Gaga. Because *indispensables* share the vision and take personal responsibility for it, they like to believe that you will take care of their growth. They are quite patient and sacrificing for the benefit of the company. The will work for lower salary and more hours than they deserve, in the hope that when the company does better, they'll do better. I found that my plans for their growth- in salary and learning curve- had to always be more than they expected.

My plan for their growth had to be bigger than their

aspirations.

In an industry where annual increase of 10% in salary is common, my *indispensables* have received 40-60% increases. They received bonuses during the worst times for the company. They get opportunities to attend workshops, conferences, and exhibitions even those beyond what's directly relevant to the company. The continued faith of *indispensables* in me is my greatest asset. I do whatever I can to keep that intact.

Oh, and there's one more. Just a quick one. This Lady Gaga stuff broke down pretty quickly. Show them off. Nothing gives greater satisfaction to an *indispensable* than your pride in them. And nothing conveys pride better than showing them off in front of customers, partners, consultants, and anyone else that matters. It's much more effective than saying *thank you* or *good work* multiple times a day.

Show off your indispensables.

So, *three good ones to stay.* Not too bad.

The Ummm's- A special breed

You know the thing about fatalism, though. It's persistent. And never more so than with Ummm's. They cover a slim spectrum between replaceable and indispensable. The worst are the ones closest to the *indispensables* but yet not one of them. They're a little too distant to be indispensable and too good to be replaceable. They don't cause a hole in the heart, more of a severe heartburn.

So, I also needed an approach to mitigate the risks of *ummm's* leaving. The days after their departure hurt with trying to figure out how the work is going to get done now that they aren't around. I had also come up with policies of *no exit interview* and *no notice period*. Once someone submits a resignation, there is no discussion. More on that in *Conflictorium*. And the worst part is that when *ummm's* leave, they shake *indispensables* too. These two groups function like one and when the *ummm* leaves, the *indispensable* has to deal with the emotions as well as the burden of handling the extra responsibilities. It's not uncommon for an *indispensable* to quit soon after an *ummm*. And that just hurts the most.

So, I needed a process of risk mitigation. I needed a plan to overcome the paranoia of dealing with the fear of a heartburn when, despite my best efforts, one of the *ummm's* decides to leave. Complicated, I know!

I came up with a two-point strategy:

· There should be an *indispensable* in every function of the company
· *Indispensables* should be involved in roles other than their primary function

The first helps manage the stress of an *ummm* leaving. Since an *indispensable* is already in the same function, taking over is easier. The second helps other *indispensables* assist in fulfilling the additional responsibilities. I have engineers handling tender bidding processes, sales guys handling aspects of accounting and quality assurance, admin guys handling aspects of production. If an *indispensable* leaves, another steps in. If there's a shortage of *indispensables*, I take up that responsibility. This strategy worked really well when dealing with Mr. S (discussed in *Chor Chor Mausere Bhai*).

I haven't been worried about someone leaving for months now. *Sigh*

16

Conflictorium

On dealing with conflict within the company

Conflictorium is a 'museum of conflict' in Ahmedabad. Their website describes them as an 'interactive museum with exhibits designed to facilitate dialogue about historical conflicts via art'. For me, the place is a haven where I could spend hours in total silence, and leave being completely moved. They say on their website, "Conflict is integral to life, but how a society manages conflicts reveals how mature it is."

> *Conflict is integral to every organization and team. There simply is no growth without conflict.*

Cool, that's simple enough. And I wish things could be left at that.

But with a conflict comes the need to manage it. With maturity.

And who knows how that is done. Talking helps, and doesn't. Explicitly placing trust in people to manage it among them-selves helps, and doesn't. Ignoring helps, never! Conflicts have arisen on a variety of issues:

- *'He uses my phone charger without asking and never gives it back on time'*
- *'She didn't speak to that customer properly'*
- *'He doesn't give me the respect I deserve'*
- *Everything in between and beyond.*

After months of dealing with this, I'd had enough of this shit and decided I wouldn't spend any time managing conflicts. Yes, you're right. That was the stupidest thing I could have done. Every time someone came to me with a complaint about another, I would shoo them away telling them to deal with it. My usual responses were:

- *'Please don't be a child about this'*
- *'You guys figure it out'*
- *'Respect is commanded not demanded'*

If you're cringing, especially to the last one, I wish you were there to help me then. I cringe thinking about that time too. What was worse was that with every repeat incident, my voice got louder, gaze more stern, and response more curt. I look back at that time with utter disappointment- a time when I feel I'd most let down my team.

As an introvert, interacting with people is generally difficult for me. On the rare occasion that I'm at a social gathering, I'm the one sitting in a corner scribbling rubbish onto a paper napkin, looking like I am coming up with a way to generate electricity from the flapping of bird wings. And two people, sitting in front of me, complaining about each other, unable to move on—there's nothing worse to look at!

It took me time to realize that people coming to me with an issue didn't do so because they were immature. They did so because, however seemingly trivial, it was something that bothered them deeply. I empathise with people whose chargers are taken without information and not returned. Try doing that with my notebook and I'll go berserk. I've been under the pressure of converting a customer and it would piss me off if someone jeopardized that, even if unknowingly. And no one wants to feel that they aren't respected. As someone in his late twenties, running a fledgling business to compete with stalwarts who've been around for longer than I've been alive, working with a team with an average age of 40, I know what it feels like to not be taken seriously, to not be respected.

I realized that lack of empathy wasn't my problem. What got to me the most was that the problem seemed unsolvable. I felt inept to handle such situations. I was trying to avoid them, blaming people of immaturity. I was under tremendous self-inflicted pressure to have all the answers, to come up with all the solutions.

What worked was a simple question: *how can we resolve this?* Not trying to find an answer by myself but doing it together as a team. Every time there was a conflict, I'd sit with the relevant people, state to them explicitly that they were each very important to me and that I wanted us to be able to work well together, and then ask them: *how can we resolve this?*

In most cases, it works. And I'm happy because it's dramatically better than my close to zero score before. They propose a solution, I add to it if I have something to say, and we try it out. If it doesn't work, we go at it again.

One time, our head of maintenance, Sudeep, came to me complaining about the fact that one of the workers wasn't taking his instructions seriously. We did the same exercise. They went out seemingly happy. Until Sudeep came back a few days later with a similar complaint about the same person. And then another a few weeks later. Both of us noticed the pattern.

So, I called Sudeep in to discuss this. He knew what the crux of the problem was. It was me. I was doing something that had caused this pattern to emerge. He explained to me that every time he confronts a worker not following his instructions or not doing the work properly, the worker retorts, "*Main sir se baat kar lunga (I will speak to Sir directly)*."

My policy of open-door and transparent communication had come back to bite me in the backside. I also had a habit of quick decision-making so I would quickly resolve the issue. No matter whose favour the decision was in, Sudeep, one of my *indispensables*, felt overstepped by the worker and mistrusted by me. I asked Sudeep to propose a solution, making it clear that it was also important to me to not sever lines of communication with workers. Sudeep understandingly proposed that every time a worker comes to me with an issue, I should call him and let the instructions be passed via him. We tried it and it worked wonders! Conflicts decreased dramatically.

Transparency can breed mistrust when employees start misusing it.

Another time, a sales executive timidly shared with me that our material had been rejected by a major customer due to quality issues. The sales, production, and quality teams huddled into my office and my otherwise perfect solution of asking *how do we resolve this* fell flat on its face. The question sparked an unending blame game. 'I had told them', 'no one ever told me', 'the sales team should get proper specs of the customer's requirement', 'the quality team should regularly check the instruments', 'the production team should give proper details', and so on. And on and on. One question, multiple problems, even more solutions. My solution had a flaw. And the modification required was:

I don't care whose fault it is. How do we resolve this?

For certain, it was someone's fault. Maybe everyone's. Maybe only mine. But it was more important to resolve the issue. And, like I've mentioned before, no one needs to feel worse than how they're already feeling about making a mistake. Especially in situations where people know whose fault it is, the person who made the mistake is feeling terrible and vulnerable. Making them feel worse doesn't help anyone. It only breeds more conflict.

The team and I have been more at peace since acknowledging that I don't have all the answers and don't care whose mistake it was. I only want to work with the team to find a solution. Not that there aren't incidents of shit hitting the fan, we're just more focused on cleaning the shit as a team than analyzing the shit. After the cleaning, the analysis becomes easier and less conflict-prone.

Focus on cleaning the shit as a team before trying to analyse the shit.

Finally, there are times when nothing works. I give it all I can but one's ego is irreparably wounded or another's sentiments hurt or yet another just found a much higher-paying opportunity. And, well, nothing can be done. The only result is a letter of resignation.

There are two rules I follow in such situations:

1. No exit interview
2. No notice period

I think exit interviews are over-rated. If something needs to be done or talked about, it should have been done before the resignation arrived. People are mostly unhelpful in exit interviews, anyway. They tend to be overly nice to get a good recommendation. If a resignation reaches me, either I have failed or they did. If I failed, I'll work on it. If they did, well, they have their life to think about it.

The *no notice period* policy is basically because that person sticking around just makes everyone gloomy. It's just..bleh. Employees are given a salary for their 'notice period' but asked to not come in.

I came to use these policies mainly because I've seen people trying to use a resignation as a tool for negotiation for a higher salary, incentives, cake or whatever the hell they wanted. And whatever comes out of it will feel like a compromise to either or both. I hate compromises.

In fact, I follow a similar policy for hiring. The rule here is:

Never ask for a time commitment

Many companies I know have bonds or other fancy terms tying in employees for a number of months or years. I don't care about that. If someone wants to leave after a few months or years or decades, either I failed or they did.

17

Market ki maar

On understanding the market you operate in

The market for our product in India can be summarized to three terms that would scare away any level-headed investor or entrepreneur:

- High saturation
- Low differentiation
- High fragmentation

Yes, the sob story continues.

A highly saturated market for a product is one in which the demand for the product has plateaued i.e. there is no significant growth in consumption of the product. While there isn't any specific data I could find to confirm this, it can be estimated by the fact that very few new companies have entered this market over the past few years. The scenario is similar on a global level. Companies which are growing are doing so mainly by acquisition instead of establishing new manufacturing units.

Low differentiation means that it is difficult to distinguish between the same product from competing companies. Been checking out laptops recently? Then you know what I'm talking about. This situation leads to high price sensitivity and ever-dropping margins. The customer knows that they can buy from any of the suppliers and each supplier is in a constant price war. There are no loyal customers.

A highly fragmented market indicates that there are many players in the market with no one having enough market share to influence the industry in a particular direction. The largest seller of our product in India has less than 15% market share. There are a few sellers in the 10% range. And then hundreds below them.

> *Kehne ko yeh market hai...Sirf kehne ko..Par idhar jungle ka kanoon chalta hai maloom. Cheenti ko Bistuiya kha jaata hai..Bistuiya ko mendhak..Mendhak ko saanp nigal jaata hai..Nevla saanp ko maarta hai..Bhediya nevle ka khoon chus leta hai..Sher bhediye ko chaba jata hai..Idhar har taqatwar apne se kam ko maarkar jeeta hai. – Vijay Deenanath Chauhan on the market situation*

You think that's it? You should know better by now.

The market is also majorly trader-driven, highly import-dependent, and has long credit cycles. I estimate that almost

70% of our product is sold to consumers by traders and not manufacturers. This means that there is a layer between the customer and manufacturer, driving prices up for the former and down for the latter. Their presence is almost ubiquitous. Manufacturers have had to shut down warehouses at different locations because they couldn't compete with the traders.

Traders create tiny kingdoms of influence. They are close to consumers, can spend more time and energy on influencing their decisions, and can supply material at short notice due to geographical proximity. And they don't have to deal with the troubles of manufacturing the product. In fact, I've met traders who have been selling our product for over a decade and didn't know how it's made.

When I say 'high import-dependency', you think China. No surprises there. Chinese companies primarily cater to the lower segment of customers and account for 40-50% of the material consumed in India. Import from other countries such as Thailand, Korea, South Africa, and others accounts for ~20%. That leaves Indian manufacturers such as us producing only 30-40% of the domestic demand. We've all read how difficult it is to compete with China in manufacturing. The traders know this better than us. So, if we can't drop our prices low enough, the trader just gets the material from China.

What this has also done is conditioned end consumers to not care much about quality. The large majority of material from China is inferior in quality to that of Indian manufacturers. But customers are used to that quality and the price point. Due to low technical differentiation, it's hard to convince customers to pay just slightly extra for our product.

I already covered the point about credit cycles in *Lohe Ke Daane Ka Dhandha*. But I'm not one to lose an opportunity to gain more sympathy (*puppy eyes*). When selling to end consumers, we get paid, on average, about 45 days from the date of delivery. Traders generally pay sooner, within 15 days on average. In the latter case, however, margins are terrible. We get a margin of roughly 20% from consumers and less than 5% from traders.

Also, because our product is an industry consumable, price increase is rare and minimal. What that means is that when prices of raw materials drop, such as during a slump, customers are quick to demand price cuts. But when prices of raw material are rising, such as the seemingly good time after a slump, the price of our product doesn't increase proportionately.

So, in a slump, we make greater losses due to decreased production leading to higher unit costs. And when the market starts getting better, we make losses due to increasing cost of raw material. If you're feeling sorry for me, do that for a few more minutes before going ahead.

Alright, I'd said in *Lohe Ke Daane* that I'll discuss the advantages of this situation. And I take my promises for silver linings very seriously. I'm happy for you to take some time to let your sympathies for me sink in deeper. When you're ready, let's dive in.

The flipside to all of the above problems are as below:

1. High saturation is an entry barrier. Because the market is already saturated, you can be comfortable that you know most of your competitors. There are no new ones springing up as is common in high growth industries.

2. Low differentiation makes you obsess over customer service. It becomes the only differentiator.

3. High fragmentation begs consolidation. Most consumers want to buy directly from manufacturers. It's more cost-effective, quality concerns are resolved better, and consistency is maintained. In a highly fragmented market, consumers are in want for a strong, trustworthy brand.

4. A trader-driven market is a boon in disguise. It tells you that the channels to all potential customers have mostly been established. We need to figure out a way to use those channels to our benefit. A solution could, therefore, be scaled very quickly.

5. High import dependency, well, I'm rooting for Make In India! That aside, it leaves room to figure out how your product or service can offer unique value to your customers. It's a chance to dig deeper to understand the pulse of the customer and solve for pain points that foreign companies might be oblivious to.

6. Long credit cycles don't have a silver lining. Accept it. Move on. Don't expect me to find a positive side to everything. A few solutions such as invoice discounting exist but they are half-baked. SME finance is a national

problem.

Let me point out here that there's always a good reason to do deep market research. More often than not, the reason emerges after the research is done.

I once watched a great talk by Peter Thiel on Youtube. It's called *How To Start A Startup: Competition Is For Losers*. In it, he talks about how to select which ideas to work on and which to absolutely stay away from. He distinguishes any company as either a monopolist or non-monopolist. Monopolists are those operating in relatively small markets, with high market share. Non-monopolists are those operating in huge markets with many competitors and low margins. And non-monopolists are basically losers! Take a guess which bracket our company falls in.

It took me quite some time to recover from this realization. It can't go down well with anyone to be called a loser by Peter Thiel. Ours is a niche industry and not a lot of data exists. But whatever existed, I needed to know. Don't wait to be called a loser before you start doing market research.

The better I knew the market conditions, the better I could face the difficulties we were operating in, and the more I could come up with workable strategies to transform the business.

18

Muft, muft, muft!

On mentors

There is a minor sect of consultants that like to refer to themselves as *mentors*. They are the most dangerous of them all.
Have you ever been to a palmist? Or an astrologist? Did they
say you were on a search for happiness? Did they tell you how
your life is full of struggles but you seem to have the grit to pull
through? Did they talk about a future illness that you'll have to
battle? And it seemed bang on. Except everyone who goes to a
palmist hears the same story. How many of us think that our
life is struggle-free? Who's not searching for happiness? And
you're going to get sick some day with your current lifestyle,
just face it.

But because they sit there, holding your hand, looking into your
eyes, it feels special. You're not special. Most *mentors* have the
same modus operandi. They're in the business of seemingly *free*

advice. You know what you should do to make your grocery shop more successful? Use technology. Build an app with artificial intelligence to automate the ordering process such that every time the baby thinks of cereal, the app orders it and it arrives before the mother has realized her baby was hungry. Then, introduce some circular economy. Also, have you heard about mixed reality? No? Let me tell you about how it's transforming the world and, implicitly, how much of an idiot you are to be spending time worrying about unit economics of your shop.

Be creative. Think outside the box. Draw a small circle, then a bigger concentric circle. The small circle is your comfort zone. Get out of it! And the vague crap goes on and on as hordes of emotionally vulnerable teenagers line up in the college auditorium to listen to this fake messiah.

They take on tags of *motivational speaker, startup mentor, business coach, elephant whisperer*, or whatever the hell they call themselves to get you to listen. Why would they lie to you when the advice is free? Well, it's not free. You're just not the one paying. Not with money, anyway. They're getting paid by your college, or YouTube, or Santa for coaching his elves to become better employees. More importantly, and herein lies the trick, they are not lying. They're just sputtering utterly vague, useless information that can be interpreted in a variety of ways, one of which will apply to you. Who figures that way out? You.

And what about all those people who became millionaires and swear by this person? They'd have become millionaires anyway. I am yet to find a mentor who shares data on how many people succeeded out of the total number of people they mentored.

They use *survivorship bias* to their advantage, sharing anecdotes of and interviewing successful people they had an 'out of the box' conversation with many years ago, leading us to believe that their quick advice was game-changing.

What about mentors who *have been* entrepreneurs? Well, if they were good at it, they wouldn't be a *'have been'.* Unless they are talking about their mistakes, don't waste any time listening to them.

Most of the 'mentors' I have met didn't know beyond the first page of the book they were quoting. They are full of inspirational quotes and anecdotes to use as filler material to hide their incompetence and pointlessness. It led me to come up with the following principle:

Nothing is better than something

Half knowledge is dangerous. Half mentorship even more so. Half mentorship is the kind described above - vague statements (*think outside the box*), connected to a pipe dream (*million dollar company*), with no actionable points (*figure it out*).

There's another type of mentor that's quite insidious. These find you once your company starts doing reasonably well. They always have a novel plan of how to invest your money to quadruple it, without any effort. Specifically, without any effort on their part. They met a person who knows someone who is already doing it and now has three Porsches, four bungalows, and five great danes, or something to that effect. These leeches have caused many successful business persons to fail miserably.

Stay away from them.

The problem, however, is not the mentors. They are a symptom. The problem is our own impatience. We want the short cut. We want quick answers. We want someone to tell us the *right* way.

And in the words of the great life coach, Hozier:

> "Would things be easier if there was a right way,
>   Honey, there is no right way."

The only *right* way is your way that worked out. No one knows what that way is. In fact, you build the way as you walk on it. The sooner we accept this, the earlier we insulate ourselves from mentors taking us away from the *right* way.

Possibly the greatest mentor and philosophical thinker of our times, Captain Barbosa, famously told his crew on a life-threatening voyage:

> "For certain you have to be lost
>   To find a place that cannot be found
>   Else ways, everyone would know
>   Where it was."

It's not surprising to me that most of my mentors are either fictional characters or people who don't know of my existence. I have never met them, only read what they've written and listened to what they said. They don't come back looking for credit when things work out or blame me for incompetence when I fail to execute their seemingly brilliant ideas.

Of those alive, and knowing of my existence, I've found the best mentors doing the following:

- They listen more than they talk- In fact, I have a hypothesis that there is an inverse law between how soon a person cuts you off and how good their advice will be i.e. the sooner a person cuts you off, the shittier their advice will be.
- They don't care to give you answers- They openly acknowledge that they don't know the answers and that you, working on this problem on the ground, are in the best position to find the answers.
- They ask a lot of questions- They want to help you find out missing gaps in your understanding of the problem.

I had no experience of this before I had the good fortune, as a college student, to spend ten minutes with Clayton Christensen. He listened to me intently as I explained to him my desire to become an entrepreneur to create solutions to a problem I was deeply affected by. And then he asked me questions- first to understand the problem better, then to understand why I wanted to work on it, how I was thinking of developing the solution, *have you thought of this, how are you thinking about solving that.*

Those ten minutes are a precious memory I often replay in my head. Mostly because, as one of the world's leading management thinkers, I didn't expect him to care so much. I have rarely found a person who *cared*. When I find such a person, I don't let them go.

Because that's what makes the best mentor. They *care*. Not by saying it. But by listening deeply. By working with you to find gaps. By acknowledging that that's the best they can do. If they work with you over a long period, they come up with actionable insights and take responsibility for walking with you through their execution.

That can't be faked.

Let me conclude this chapter with a quote by Brene Brown that beautifully sums up how I look for a mentor:

> "If you're not in the arena also getting your ass kicked, I'm not interested in your feedback."

19

Ek Chutki Innovation Ki Keemat

On the importance of innovation

Dylan Moran is one of my favourite stand-up comedians. He is my soul brother, if ever there was such a thing. He once said that life has four stages- child, failure, old, dead. And I identify with that. I've spent much of my adolescence and adulthood failing. And the constant sense of failure became so much more acute once I started running a business. It became a daily occurrence. Moran has some ideas on how we, differently for men and women, try to escape this sense of failure and impending death. It's hilarious, you should check it out.

> *I believe that the stages of a company's life can similarly be reduced to- child, failure, innovating, dead.*

Everyday the company doesn't innovate, it's either a failure or closer to death. And by innovation, I don't mean coming up with the next iPhone. I just mean coming up with solutions that are novel to your company or industry and that give you a competitive advantage. There's a lot of debate on the differences between *jugaad* and innovation. My point is that it doesn't matter as long as it gives me a competitive advantage.

And it's a myth that innovation happens only in big companies. You've read the stories of how most highly successful, innovative companies started in garages or dorm rooms. And they became successful by displacing prevailing industry leaders.

Now, I don't know if there is a process to coming up with successful innovations. I can't seem to find anyone else who has a clue either. But there are a few tools (links mentioned in *Kaam Ki Cheezein*) I like to use when thinking of ideas:

- Lean Canvas- There are multiple versions of this. I like the one developed by Ash Maurya, available on his platform, Lean Stack. The Lean Canvas is a great way to break down any business idea into simple components that help you think about all things relevant to making the idea work.
- Lean Startup methodology- Popularised by Eric Ries, this methodology follows an iterative cycle of build-measure-learn. Each iteration helps develop a better version of the solutions. The faster the iterations, the quicker you get to a fully-working solution.
- Design Toolkit- Developed by Ideo, a pioneer in product design (they designed Apple's first mouse), this contains a set of helpful tools to create what they call 'human-centered design'. Replace 'human' with 'customer' and the toolkit will help you come up with the right questions

to get answers to when developing your solution.

When it comes to ideas, I am a quantity-over-quality kind of person. I don't know if that's a good thing. Linus Pauling ("If you want to have good ideas, you must have many ideas") and Adam Grant (author of *Originals*) seem to approve. And I am happy in my *confirmation bias*.

The lean canvas and design thinking toolkit help me weed out many ideas so that I can focus my energy on ones that seem to at least work on paper. Then, starts the fuzzy process of developing the solution. I try to practice the build-measure-learn cycle with as much pace as I can. That helps further shortlist ideas and come up with refinements. This has never been a linear process. Honestly, it would be much less fun for me if it was.

Below are three examples of when this kind of thinking helped us.

1. *Chitthi* - B2B marketing is an annoying term. Anyone who deals with it, knows. Most marketing strategies have been developed for B2C marketing. There are platforms such as IndiaMart, Trade India, Alibaba. They work sometimes, mostly not. We had a list of potential customers and we did whatever came to mind- created a website, started a Facebook business page, cold emails and calls, created profiles on IndiaMart et al, banged our heads against the wall, everything.

   None of our potential customers seem to like Facebook

for business. Phone numbers were mostly wrong. How many unread emails do you have in your inbox? Our potential customers too, apparently. The IndiaMart stuff was more an annoyance than anything else. Ours is a niche product, the leads were just not relevant. Banging our heads, well, that's not a sustainable option. And we didn't have the budget to spend on participating in exhibitions across the country or send our sales team on door-to-door marketing. In fact, in two years, we didn't participate in a single exhibition. Our sales mostly grew through customer referrals but it wasn't good enough.

After months of *failing*, we had an idea. Aman and I were engaged in our almost daily late-evening chat when the postman arrived. It was unusually late for him but he said he had to finish his quota for the day. Soon after the letter arrived, it came into my hands, and then got passed on to the relevant person for further action. A letter! You don't get many of those nowadays, do you? And you always open them! Aman and I realised that it was the only form of communication that always found its way to me.

So, we started sending out letters. Like the one you sent when you were 13. Wait, that had hearts and glitter on it. Not that kind. Phone numbers change, company addresses rarely do. Emails are ignored, letters rarely so. We sent out over 150 letters in a week. Within a month, we got three positive leads, and a confirmed order. We spent Rs. 4000 on this marketing strategy. Got a confirmed order of Rs. 11.5 lakh. Pretty good, right?

2. *Lakdi* – The credit for this goes entirely to Aman. Firewood was used at the factory for heating some parts relevant to handling molten metal. This is critical because the molten metal is at a temperature of ~1600° C. After months of frustration with the growing local unavailability of firewood, Aman came to me with the idea of creating an LPG-fired, open oven for the same purpose. LPG is much more easily available, is a better (economical and environment-friendly) fuel, and easier to store and handle.

He discussed with the mechanical maintenance team, drew out a plan to build it, got it built within a week using mostly parts and components lying around the factory, tested it, made a few modifications, and forever rid us of our dependency on firewood. His machine cost us about Rs. 10,000 to make and saves us about Rs. 4,000 per month in direct expenses. Indirectly, it saved us lakhs. See, when we used firewood, the heating was not uniform and it was difficult to assess whether the part would hold at the high temperature when it interacts with the hot metal. It had caused leakages in the past. Imagine your tap leaking water at 1600° C. Not fun. One leakage could cause a loss of about Rs. 60,000 in material and resources. It was also a major safety hazard.

Sometimes, we get so focused on the new that we don't stop to question the old. He questioned, innovated, and solved. Also, he solved 5 issues in quality, safety, procurement, purchase, and inventory management; by solving one of them. That's a good example of the 80/20 principle, which is quite common with innovation.

3. *Kachra* – This was one that demanded the entire gamut of tools at our disposal. After reading *Market Ki Maar* and *Lohe Ke Daane Ka Dhandha*, you know our business and the kind of market we operate in. We spent almost a year continually brainstorming on how to differentiate our offerings but in vain. The only tool for every player in the industry was pricing. But margins are really low, so we couldn't reduce our prices further.

So, almost a year went by in rants, ramblings, and tears. There seemed to be no solution. Until one day, while talking to the purchase manager of a company, I happened to ask, "What do you do with our material after it is used?" He was a little taken aback. He had no clue. So, I got back to him a few days later, after he had spoken to his production team. He told me that, mostly, the material is thrown away. The majority of steel in the world is recycled. Not our product, not in an organized manner anyway.

I started wondering if we could start recycling the product. After our product is used, what is left behind is a powdered mixture of steel and other impurities. I asked the purchase manager to send us a sample, and he did.

Over the next few months, the team led by Sudeep and Aman worked with me to develop a process of recycling and value addition of this steel powder, using principles of circular economy and mechanical engineering.

We became the first manufacturer of our kind in the world to offer a buy-back guarantee on the waste generated from the use of our product. It has enabled us to differentiate ourselves, increase market penetration, and generated savings that helped us survive the auto industry crisis of 2019. Many of our competitors shut shop in the same period. We are also applying for three patents, based on our solution.

The above examples could come under various categories of business management mumbo jumbo- process innovation, business model innovation, product innovation, sales innovation, etc. I'd like to say that we are naturally innovative and experimental and exploratory and other fancy words to describe inventive geniuses.

The truth is, we just keep trying to delay being dead.

20

Meri Phat Rahi Hai

On being vulnerable

Running a business is tough. And the toughest part is keeping a strong face through it all. Because you have a team that, at best, understands the pains you're going through but still has only you to look up to for strength and confidence. The only thing that keeps them going is their belief in you. So, you smile through the pain, go into the washroom, cry your heart out, puke your brains out, and come back with the same smile you left with.

It's tough.

You wish you could be more openly vulnerable. In her beautiful Ted Talk, Brene Brown talks about the 'power of vulnerability'. There are some things you can and should do.

Be more open about admitting your mistakes. Your team will have more trust and respect towards you.

Be more open to making mistakes, making a fool out of yourself, feeling rejection and pain, accepting failure as something that's part of every journey.

If you aren't doing these already, there's a good chance you'd have learnt by yourself. I might have, at the most, prompted you to do the above with active intent. And you might have already seen the results. You feel lighter, more in control, more empowered.

But you want to climb to the top of the building and scream, "*Meri phat rahi hai!!*" That, you can't do. Your heart feels like it's going to leap out of your mouth. Maybe you are having a panic attack. But you dare not show it. Not to everyone. Not to those who depend on you for their salaries. Those you consider family.

And not to your blood family, of course. They didn't want you to get into business in any case. Or, worse still, you got into business *for* them. You don't want them to know how hard this really is. Your friends can't understand. They try, genuinely. But they can't.

There have been times when I would sit in the verandah of my apartment. For the whole night. Staring into the darkness. Trying to silently fight the terrible sinking feeling I was being crushed by. At 4 am, I'd finally muster just enough energy to fall into my bed. When I'd wake up, with every step, my mind would shout, "Run away!"

On my way to work, I'd pause at the railway crossing and imagine what it would be like to just get on the train. And leave. Forget about everything I was going through. All these things I couldn't speak to anyone about.

It's a high price. You'd read enough about how difficult it is to get the business right. But no one ever told you how bloody lonely it was going to be. And now you don't know what to do about it.

I don't have the answer. I don't know if entrepreneurship can be less lonely. But I know there are things that made me feel more lonely than I needed to.

Top among them- the critics. That wonderfully useless group of people, picking apart at your personal and professional life. *You need work-life balance, this is not sustainable. How could you be so stupid as to trust that person? What the hell were you thinking when you took that highly risky bet?*

Mr. Roosevelt, help me out please:

> "It is not the critic who counts; not the [person] who points out how the strong [person] stumbles, or where the doer of deeds could have done them better. The credit belongs to the [person] who is actually in the arena, whose face is marred by dust and sweat and blood; who strives valiantly; who errs, who comes short again and again, because there is

no effort without error and shortcoming; but who does actually strive to do the deeds; who knows great enthusiasms, the great devotions; who spends [themself] in a worthy cause; who at the best knows in the end the triumph of high achievement, and who at the worst, if [they] fail, at least fail while daring greatly, so that [their] place shall never be with those cold and timid souls who neither know victory nor defeat."

Get the critics out of your head, out of your life. But before that let me give them a piece of my mind.

Work-life balance is for losers. It's for people who don't pursue either with a passion. Here's what Picasso said about his desire to paint:

"If they took away my paints I'd use pastels. If they took away my pastels I'd use crayons. If they took away my crayons I'd use pencils. If they stripped me naked and threw me in prison I'd spit on my finger and paint on the walls."

Want to lecture him on work-life balance? Be my guest. And you know why you think I don't have work-life balance. It's because I have no time for you– you sad, annoying, little piece of shit! I put my time and energy into relationships I value. I make time to spend with my family and a few friends who understand my purpose in life. And I'd rather sit in a pool of dung, playing with cockroaches than spend more time with you.

Also, I trusted *that* person because I have the courage to do so. More than you can claim for anything you have done in your life. I took *that* risky bet because I have confidence in myself. I know it went wrong, I learnt my lesson, and next time I will work harder.

Wait, wait. It's not over. Dear Mr. Jordan, your turn:

> "Look me in the eyes.
>   It's okay if you're scared,
>   So am I.
>   But we're scared for different reasons.
>   I'm scared of what I won't become,
>   and you're scared of what I could become.
>   Look at me.
>   I won't let myself end where I started,
>   I won't let myself finish where I began.
>   I know what is within me,
>   Even if you can't see it yet.
>   Look me in the eyes.
>   I have something more important than courage,
>   I have patience.
>   I will become,
>   what I know I am."

How scared are you, really? I know you're scared that you'll never find something to pursue with as much passion as I do with my work. You will never know what it is like to burn with the fire of trying to solve a problem that can impact actual lives.

And, finally, *Naniji:*

"Jab tak jalega nahi, sona kaise banega"

I am willing to go through the fire even if it has the slightest possibility that I could come out as pure gold. I am willing to take that risk. I am ready to put myself on the line. Are you?

No. So, shut the fuck up and go find a rock to live under.

Aahhh! That felt good! And serves as a good segue to my next point- honesty.

I wasn't honest about who I needed out of my life. Some people aren't worth it. They want you to be normal i.e. less passionate, less driven, less you. And it took me too long to decide that these people didn't deserve to be in my thoughts, much less a part of my life.

The funny thing? When these people were gone, I suddenly had more time for my family. For friends who cared about me. Until then, these people sucked all my time and energy. And made me more and more lonely.

When I tell my friends that I am going off-grid for a while (like when I decided to write this book), they accept it. They know I need time to deal with my stuff. When I am ready, I will talk about it. The people worth keeping are the people who wait for me, as narcissistic as that may sound, because they value our relationship.

They *don't* understand what I'm going through. But they trust me to get through it. With their help if I ask for it. Without it, if

I don't. It's important to fill our lives with the few people who will stand by us even if they don't understand.

They're the ones, the only ones, I call just to say, *"Meri phat rahi hai.."* If you've found them, be grateful. If not, don't stop looking.

Then comes being honest to ourselves. Look, we made a *choice*. We chose to run a business. If anyone told you it was going to be easy, they lied. If you thought it was a straight path to success, you were wrong. Get over it. Stop trying to convince yourself that the world is uniquely unfair towards you. It's unfair to everyone. Which is why so few people make the choice you did. Stop reading about success stories, looking for justification of how it was easier for that person. Look deeper, be uncomfortable about the fact that those successful people put in extraordinary effort to achieve what they have.

Something made you take the leap- blind optimism, desire for wealth or impact, dream to buy a swanky chocolate truffle cake and eat it by yourself, whatever it might be. Hold on to it. You're going to need it. Don't let people waver you from your goal and motivations. That just makes you weaker and lonelier. Get rid of those people.

And if you're going to give up, just give up and move on. I get it, sometimes it gets too difficult to breathe. Sometimes, you have to move on so that you can get back to it at a better time. And that better time may be never. Maybe you realized that running a business is just not what you want to do. Just move on.

If you can't or won't, stop whining and get on with it. Just spare everyone, especially yourself, the 'to be or not to be' crap.

Kaam ki cheezein

The following are books and tools I engage with regularly in my work.

Books

1. The Little Prince- Antoine de Saint-Exupery, because life is about a little more than your work and 'it is only with the heart that one can see clearly; what is essential is invisible to the eye'.
2. How Will You Measure Your Life- Clayton Christensen, because someday you'd want to measure it
3. The Essential Drucker- Peter Drucker, on almost all topics of significance to any business person (special chapter recommendation: Managing Oneself)
4. The Art Of Thinking Clearly- Rolf Dobeli, on why we make utterly dumb decisions
5. Lean Startup- Eric Ries, on principles the *B Gang* loves
6. The $100 Startup- Chris Guillebeau, on thinking about how to start a business and what ideas to work on
7. What You Do Is Who You Are- Ben Horowitz, on how to build the right culture within your organization
8. Romancing The Balance Sheet- Anil Lamba, on the most important finance-related stuff you'd need to know to run your business

9. Zero To One– Peter Thiel, for a kick in the right place when you are not thinking of innovation
10. The Innovator's Dilemma– Clayton Christensen, for a lesson on 'death without innovation' and feeling good about your small business

Free/Inexpensive Tools

1. Lean Canvas– www.leanstack.com/leancanvas, for assessing new ideas
2. Design Toolkit– www.ideo.com/post/design-kit, for coming up with new ideas
3. Wix– www.wix.com, for building quick, simple websites
4. Zoho– www.zoho.com, for online accounting, inventory management, customer management, and many other useful tools
5. Glide Apps– www.glideapp.com, for building simple mobile apps using just a Google Sheet
6. Google Docs, Sheets, Slides– drive.google.com, for collaborative documents
7. Google Forms– www.google.com/forms/, for creating online survey forms (such as for customer and employee feedback)
8. Canva– www.canva.com, for creating posters, flyers, brochures, visiting cards
9. Google Data Studio– datastudio.google.com, for creating interactive online dashboards (such as to present data in front of customers) using Google Sheets
10. Google Jamboard, Sketchboard, Conceptboard– 'Connect more apps' within Google Drive, for brainstorming with your team using an online whiteboard

Alvida

I was told that I should have a concluding chapter- that all the preceding stories should finally be tied into a beautiful, closing narrative.

I think closures are overrated. And as much as our brain would like to find beautiful patterns to 'connect the dots', I don't think most dots connect anyway. They pop up at random moments in life and we'd like them to fit in. But they don't. It makes us crazy to not have a pattern.

Here's a quote from Milan Kundera:

"There is no means of testing which decision is better, because there is no basis for comparison. We live everything as it comes, without warning, like an actor going on cold. And what can life be worth if the first rehearsal for life is life itself? That is why life is always like a sketch. No, "sketch" is not quite the word, because a sketch is an outline of something, the groundwork for a picture, whereas the sketch that is our life is a sketch for nothing, an outline with no picture."

Success in entrepreneurship, as with everything else in life I guess, comes after accepting that there is no 'sketch'. Everything I have written in this book came from no sketch. We were just living everything as it came, learning from whatever we could find, trying out as many decisions as quickly as we could, hoping a few would work. We continue to do so.

Don't let the structure of this book fool you. Our journey wasn't divided into clean parts and chapters. It was messy, frustrating, painful, and exhilarating; sometimes simultaneously. We learnt what we did during odd hours of the night, sitting on the toilet, having dinner with family, standing at the cigarette shop, staring into nothing with our heads in our hands hoping to find something hard to bang against, anytime and anywhere. We struggled every day, often late into the night. This also means that we were consumed almost completely by what we were trying to solve. We continue to be so.

Also, let me clarify that none of the solutions were 'quick' or 'final' in any sense. Most of them didn't work, those that did took unbearably long to show results. Many times, we'd have given up on a solution altogether before something clicked and it actually worked. At other times, something completely out of control changed and a solution would become more viable than it had previously been. We were constantly coming up with new solutions, assessing old ones, and juggling the two to make something work. We continue to do so.

The back-cover of this book says that it's a handbook for you. I lied. If anything, I hope you realize that the only handbook that matters is the one you make for yourself. And if a few of my chapters find a way into yours, I'll be happy.

Alvida :)

Abhyv Jahan
jahan.abhyv@gmail.com
www.loveprofitdhokha.com
lpdbook.glideapp.io

Made in the USA
Middletown, DE
23 September 2023

39170346R00102